THE NIGHTINGALE

Nightingale

THE NIGHTINGALE

ITS STORY AND SONG

AND OTHER FAMILIAR SONG-BIRDS OF BRITAIN

BY

OLIVER G. PIKE

F.Z.S., F.R.P.S., M.B.O.U.

*With 24 photographs
by the author*

ARROWSMITH : LONDON

FIRST PUBLISHED IN OCTOBER, 1932

PRINTED IN GREAT BRITAIN BY
J. W. ARROWSMITH LTD., 11 QUAY STREET, BRISTOL

FOREWORD

THERE is no country in the world so favoured as England for bird song. In other countries we find birds with wonderful plumage, birds which build more marvellous nests, and birds with very remarkable habits ; but if we search the world over, we shall never find a spot so filled with avian music as the corner of an English wood.

In preparing this book on the song-birds frequently met with, it has been my aim to assist my readers to identify them by their markings, habits and song. The descriptions of their markings have not been minutely described. I have simply given what is their general appearance to the casual observer, adding incidents from their lives and describing their song, so that when visiting the country the reader may be able to recognize them.

The photographs should also help in identifying them, they have all been taken by myself direct from wild nature.

Foreword

I am greatly indebted to my friend Mr. H. O. Oddy, of Oxford, who has assisted so much in finding suitable nests of nightingales for me to photograph.

O. G. P.

The Bungalow,
    Leighton Buzzard.

CONTENTS

LIST OF ILLUSTRATIONS

8

List of Illustrations

The Nightingale

Description.—Length, 6¼ inches. Upper parts, reddish-brown; lower part of rump and whole of tail, rich chestnut red; breast, buff-white; under parts, greyish-white; bill: upper, brown; lower, grey; legs and feet, varying from pale flesh to pale grey; eyes, dark brown and prominent.

Field Characters.— Can be distinguished by its long, rufous tail, which is moved slowly up and down just after settling, and again often before flying. Many of its actions like that of the robin, but not so rapid. When on nest the hen sits very low, with the upper part of head and long tail only showing, but the large, brilliant eye will often betray her. Found in woods with plenty of bramble undergrowth, in lanes, roadside copses, and untrimmed hedges with oaks growing near. Song described in chapter.

THE nightingale is one of the most famous British birds; its wonderful song has been broadcast on so many occasions that there are few countries in the world which have not heard it. Thousands of people in this country who live in places where the nightingale is never likely to be seen have listened to its notes. One instance stands out vividly in my mind. I was away among the hills in a lonely part of Scotland where most of the bird notes consisted of the cries of the wild moorland species; almost at midnight the familiar song came to me through my loud-speaker, the singer was nearly five hundred miles away, yet

11

nightingale, and from that time to the present day the wonderful song, coming to us through the silence and darkness, has stirred the imagination of many writers since Virgil wrote his celebrated passage :

" As the lone bird of song in poplar shades
  Bewails her ravished young, which some hard clown
Noting hath drawn, still fledglings, from their nest ;
So she weeps night-long, and from some thick bough
Again renews her strain, her strain so sad,
And fills wide silence with her sorrowing plaints."

If I were asked to select the most beautiful lines describing the nightingale's song I should without hesitation choose that simple but descriptive passage of Isaac Walton's in his *Compleat Angler,* written nearly three hundred years ago :—

" But the nightingale, another of my airy creatures, breathes such sweet, loud music out of her little instrumental throat, that it might make mankind to think miracles are not ceased. He that at midnight, when the very labourer sleeps securely, should hear, as I have very often, the clear airs, the sweet descants, the natural rising and falling, the doubling and redoubling of her voice, might well be lifted above earth, and say, Lord, what music hast thou provided for the saints in heaven, when thou affordest bad men such music on earth ! "

Nightingale.

The only criticism that I can give to either of these quotations is that the female nightingale does not sing! It is the male alone which is responsible for the beautiful music. I have often been surprised to find that many dwellers in the country, who should know better, believe that all birds sing, whereas it is only the males that give out the best music. Many of the female birds have to be content to go through their lives making few sounds, but it is surprising what a variety of small notes some of our birds have, which it is only possible to hear if you are quite close. I have spent thousands of hours during my life concealed in a hide close to our wild birds, and I have listened to some remarkable notes which have never been recorded by other naturalists. When the female nightingale brings food to her young, she announces her arrival by uttering a pleasing series of notes unlike any other sounds made by these birds. Sedge- and reed-warblers, hedge-sparrows, tree-sparrows, the tits and finches, all utter low sounds which might be likened to conversational notes while they are standing over or near their young.

In a lifetime spent among our wild birds two nightingales stand out very vividly, for both were really master singers. I was standing near an old milestone; if you went on your knees and parted the long grass you could

15

just decipher the words "London 9 miles." Before me was an old wood, a relic of the great forest over which Queen Elizabeth and her followers hunted. The crimson clouds, which showed the course of the setting sun, faded to grey, for a few fleeting moments they were lit up with that wonderful afterglow which is such a feature of some of our English sunsets, then darkness settled down and there was a silence in the wood. Overhead heavy clouds were rolling up slowly, for no wind broke the stillness among the trees, and in such a close, damp atmosphere the very air seemed to be impregnated with the heat left behind by the departed sun. The night was as dark as it was damp and close, but the one night in a thousand to hear the nightingale at his best.

I made my way towards the wood, through long grass and under trees that seemed to stand in motionless expectancy; as I passed on through the thick undergrowth many suggestive rustlings were heard. Now it was a rabbit, then a rat, and often a shrill squeak in the grass told me that a frightened shrew was scuttling for its life. To reach the wood I had to pass across a valley which was watered by a small stream, and along the bank of this I wended my way, listening again to a medley of sounds, many of them recognized as belonging to the creatures which search for their living

16

during the hours of darkness; a loud sniff and a scuffle, and what looked like a large black ball disappeared into the night, and I knew that my careful and silent tread had surprised a badger while he was nosing in the undergrowth for food. There were bird notes high above, cries of birds of passage, and these are always fascinating, for they may belong to some interesting species that is passing over these small islands of ours on its long journey; young moorhens called from the stream, intermingled with the warning notes of their parents; many moths were out and about, and their flitting forms danced before me one second, then were lost in the darkness.

Away in the distance was a low rumbling, and the storm clouds rolled up to add to the gloom; now and again the wood was lit up with a fitful glare, as lightning which was many miles away flashed on one side of the horizon to illumine the whole heavens. It was now that grand shapes were to be seen, huge masses of clouds, one behind the other, all rolling onwards, seeming as though they were meeting above.

A large drop of rain struck a leaf, others followed, and then the stillness was broken, not by a flash and crash, but by a wonderful burst of song from my nightingale. Almost with his first notes the storm broke, and flash

were three hours to go before our troops had to attack the enemy's stronghold, and those who went through this ordeal will agree that the anxious waiting was one of the very worst features of the war. Away to the east there was the unceasing roar from a hundred guns, and nearer the sharper reports of the German shrapnel as it burst over our lines. The wood was lit up with vivid flashes, while overhead a score of star shells floated, flickered a moment or two, then died down. As the time wore on the shells increased in violence, the whole ground seemed to be trembling with the force of the explosions, when suddenly there broke out a glorious melody. At first the nightingale seemed doubtful, and there were pauses between his bursts of song, but as the bombardment increased he took up the challenge, and if we had searched the world over, it would have been difficult to have found a greater contrast than that between the beautiful harmony of his song and the awful discord of the bursting shells. But as suddenly as the song began it ceased, for a shell burst under the singer, and the tree in which it was perched was blown to matchwood, and the small bird which had entertained the waiting soldiers was killed, together with five brave men who were near.

Many other instances of nightingales singing through the most terrible bombardments came

under my notice, and I think there is little
doubt that some of them succeeded in rearing
their young in woods which were shelled almost
daily. These birds gave out their best music,
and time after time I have proved that if you
want to get the best efforts out of a nightingale
you *must* provide an opposition entertainment
that will almost drown its song. The raucous
noise of a klaxon motor-horn will often start
a bird singing. I suggest that the next time
the British Broadcasting Company attempt to
broadcast the song of the nightingale they
should provide a battery of big drums within
a hundred yards of the singer, then listeners
will hear what wonderful music this bird is
capable of giving.

Why does a nightingale sing ? When he
first arrives in this country from Africa in the
month of April two reasons induce him to
utter his loud notes. One is undoubtedly to
attract the female, and another is to announce
to all his rivals that he has taken possession
of a certain territory. Poets and other writers
delight to tell us that the bird is singing to
and soothing his mate as she sits on her nest
on the ground beneath. No doubt she likes to
hear his music, for she knows that while he
sings continuously from one perch danger is
absent ; but it is far more likely he is telling
all the other wild denizens of the wood or

21

coppice that " here I am, and here I mean to stay."

Near my home there is a large and beautiful wood in which there are about two dozen pairs of nightingales. The males appear to arrive about a week before the females, and almost as soon as they reach this northern home of theirs each male takes possession of his territory. By the behaviour and excellence of song of certain of the males I believe that a bird which owned a certain stretch of woodland last season endeavours and usually succeeds in taking possession this spring. I have studied the nightingales in this wood for several seasons, and I find that the boundaries of their territories are very clearly marked. Each patch occupied by a pair is about fifty yards square. Especially is this so on the long stretch of wood that borders the road. All through the nesting period, from the time that the birds are mated, to the time when the young are able to fly freely, they appear to keep strictly to their respective quarters. If a male belonging to one territory approaches too near another's ground the male belonging to the latter will utter a few bars of his song; if the other remains and replies he will approach it nearer, and with a loud and long period of song tries to out-sing his rival. It is at such times that I have listened to some fine singing, for when a nightingale is warning off trespassers he gives of his best. If we enter one of these territories and endeavour to drive the male away he will just travel round and inside his domain. I have never seen another male actually inside a tract of woodland belonging to a rival, so I cannot say if a fight would ensue.

When the males arrive, about the third week in April, and their territory is decided upon—and this will sometimes be settled before the females arrive about a week later—the males sing to attract a mate to their domain. When she comes, song certainly takes a large part of the actual courting, but between the bursts of song, which are often at their best at this time, the male will display before her. This courting takes place low down among the bushes and is not easy to follow; but we have seen him bowing before her, opening and spreading his fine tail, fluttering his wings, and really performing what I can only call a waltz. He sits on a branch close to her, and during the whole time is moving, not rapidly, but in a most graceful manner. The tail goes up and down as if fixed on a pivot, the head is dipped, the beak lowered far below the level of the perch; then he turns sideways, goes through the whole performance again, and from beginning to end every movement is exceedingly graceful. I have never watched a more beautiful display by any bird, every action is a joy to watch, and the long, rufous tail, raised and lowered, spread and closed, adds to a picture which remains engraved on the memory for ever. In my sound film showing the life story of the nightingale, which I obtained in the spring and early summer of 1931, I was fortunate to secure a lengthy picture of this scene, which is certainly one of the most delightful to be seen in our English woods.

It is a mistake to think that the nightingale sings only at night; far more music is given out by this woodland singer during the hours of daylight than during the night. Some nightingales will give marvellous displays of song at night, but on very many occasions I have visited well-known haunts at night and have heard very little song. At other times I have been more fortunate, and between nine o'clock and midnight have listened to some fine outbursts. Dawn, at the end of May or beginning of June, is also a good time to hear the song, but there is such a chorus of other song then that the music of the nightingale is almost lost.

I wonder how many of my readers have taken the trouble to visit any English wood to listen to the burst of song at dawn ? Those who have not done this have missed the finest

24

Two courting-display attitudes of male Nightingale

bird concert to be heard in any part of the world, for there is no country so favoured as this England of ours. We must choose the right time for our visit, and a suitable morning. A few years ago a person living in one of the British colonies travelled over three thousand miles to hear the nightingale's song, but as he arrived in England in the month of November he had a sad disappointment! The most suitable wood is that not too far from human dwellings, and the best spot in the wood is in the vicinity of a keeper's cottage. A warm morning with a clear sky is the most favourable, and the best time during the last two weeks of May and the first week of June. We should be in the wood not later than three-thirty. When we first arrive there will probably be a great silence, perhaps we hear the cry of a night bird as it travels to its roosting-place where it spends the hours of daylight, or it may be a call of a fox or badger. The sky in the east gradually becomes brighter, then a small hedge-sparrow, or a robin, or one of the lesser singers gives out a bar or two of its song, and almost immediately a great chorus of song bursts out all over the wood. It travels on like a fitful breeze that starts at one end of the wood to finish up at the other; but as this wave moves on it leaves no silence behind it, for every individual singer seems to be doing

25

such runs down the side of a wood, it is there we shall find the nests more frequently than in the wood itself.

The nest itself is a bulky one, but they vary considerably in size, some are much neater than others. The foundation consists of dead leaves, principally those of the oak, while the interior is sometimes lined with the same leaves, or a few dead grasses and hair. Some of the nests I have found have had platforms of leaves built around them, the whole harmonizing so completely with the numerous dead leaves lying around that it has not been easy to discover them.

The eggs are usually olive-green or olive-brown, with sometimes a few dark brown markings. A rare variety is bright blue, like that of the hedge-sparrow. I have seen one instance only of this remarkable clutch. Still another is a dirty white with brown markings. But out of many dozens that we may examine, the majority, quite ninety per cent., are the olive-green or olive-brown type.

The hen sits very closely upon her eggs; if we are searching for it, and happen to strike the vegetation close to her with our stick, she slips off so cunningly through the undergrowth that she often escapes unseen; at other times she will dart away above the nest, and the bright russet on the tail is all the glimpse we

have of her as she disappears among the leaves.
Very soon after she is off we hear the warning
cry—a musical whistle " pui," followed by a
deep guttural " purr." On returning to her
eggs she seldom shows herself, but just slips
cleverly through the undergrowth. Once or
twice I have seen the male bird driving her back
to her eggs, a thing that many male birds will
do when they think their mates have left their
charge long enough ; this driving usually takes
place within a few feet of the nest, and it has
always been easy to discover it after such a
scene.

If we enter a territory while the hen is
sitting, the male will first fly to meet us, then
he sings lustily to warn his mate, afterwards he
will work slowly from it, singing continuously
as we get near. We may on such occasions get
to within a couple of yards of him, and as long
as we remain there he will entertain us with
his song. I have listened to some very fine
singing when searching for the nest. The song
is undoubtedly given to warn the hen, and this
warning song is nearly always followed by some
excited whistles with the purring note following.

It is easier to discover the nest when the
young are about half-grown, for if we approach
it, say, to within thirty or forty yards, both
parents become very excited, giving out their
two warning notes every few seconds. If we

mother announces her arrival with a few low notes, " zee-zee-zee," later it is not necessary to tell them she is coming, for they either hear or see her, and up go the four or five beaks, all open widely. I do not know whether the parents use any discretion in feeding their young, or whether the food is placed into the beak nearest to them. Some birds, such as the wrens and the tits, appear to remember which young they have fed when they are outside the nest, but whether they do this inside I cannot say. I have taken several cinema films of these parents feeding their young, showing how they give each youngster a portion in turn.

I have often seen it stated that the nightingale ceases to sing after the young are out of their eggs ; this is not so, for I have often heard the male in full song during the period of feeding. In the territory which we called No. 2 a pair of nightingales built their nest at the foot of a sapling which was standing among hundreds of others ; it was really a miniature forest, with the trees so close together that we had to cut our way through ; the nest was found about three yards from the margin, in full view upon the ground, with one of the trees as a support at the back. I obtained photographs here of the parents feeding their young, and was surprised to find that on many of his visits with food the male gave out a few bars of his song. On arriving at the nest during the afternoon he had three plump green caterpillars lying across his beak. It seemed impossible for him to sing with this load of food, but he was not inconvenienced in the least, for, standing upon a twig a couple of feet above the nest, he gave a fine exhibition of singing, uttering some of his best notes.

I have often heard male birds attempting to sing with food in their beaks, but none have been so successful as this nightingale. While waiting in my hide close to a blackbird's nest I heard some remarkable sounds on my right. On looking through a peep-hole I saw the male blackbird sitting on a fence with a big bunch of worms in his beak ; with this encumbrance he attempted to sing, and the sounds that came from him sounded very much like those made by a cart wheel when in need of grease ! Many readers may think that waiting in a hide for several hours is tedious work, but really the time goes quite quickly, especially when working in a wood ; there is always so much to see and hear that our attention is taken up the whole time.

The hours spent in a hide are not wasted. Many would envy me one afternoon that I waited in my small bird-tent. As I looked through my periscope my eyes could feast themselves upon a carpet of bluebells which covered almost the whole wood, while here and there pale primroses filled up the gaps. A garden-warbler was reeling off its marvellous song close to me, four blackbirds with their deep contralto notes seemed to be holding a duel of song within a few yards of my hide, a willow-warbler with its rather monotonous undulating notes was uttering them four times every minute, a male chiff-chaff called the notes from which it derives its name incessantly, a thrush which had its nest close by was singing to its sitting mate, and right through the wood a wonderful mixed melody reached my ears; but, to crown all, a nightingale, perched on a twig just a few inches above my head, was endeavouring to drown all other singers with music that it was worth going a hundred miles to hear. For several hours this concert went on, and although no two notes were uttered in unison, and many were singing in a different key, the whole was the most perfect harmony that it was possible to listen to. It is instances like this which call the nature photographer to his work, and make the hours spent in a hide seem short.

I always attempt to build a hide in which one may be comfortable, and instead of using a peep-hole from which the view obtained is confined to perhaps just the nest we expect the bird to come to, I now use a periscope; the tube of this is very little thicker than a large fountain-pen, so it is quite inconspicuous at the top of the hide, and by turning it around one obtains a view of the whole countryside. With my periscope I have had some delightful glimpses of the home life of the nightingale, for I have been able to follow it with my eye as it travelled over its territory, watch it collecting food and bringing this to the young.

I was able to see that the birds do not travel far from their nests in search of food. In the middle of June most woods are infested with caterpillars, which are to be found on the bushes, on both tall and short trees, and on the ground. I have seen the undergrowth in our nightingale wood black with their droppings, the bramble leaves, grass and other herbage being covered with what at first glance looks like a black powder; some of the trees have their branches quite bare, showing where these injurious pests have cleared off the leaves. It was these caterpillars that the nightingales captured for their young, so we can understand that they did not have to travel far to find food.

Collectors of birds' eggs have often stated that it does no harm to take the first clutch of eggs laid by a bird, for it will build another nest and lay a second lot of eggs. The majority of birds will do this, but the robbing of the first nest makes a very great difference in the number of insect pests which will infest that bird's district in the following spring. For instance, each pair of nightingales will give their young hundreds of caterpillars each day they are in the nest, and this destruction must make a difference in the number of perfect insects which are hatched out later on, and which lay eggs to turn into caterpillars to continue their work of destruction the following spring. The collector will at once say that the nightingales would destroy just as many when feeding their second brood, but investigation proves that they do not. The life of these caterpillars is a short one, and Nature decrees that the nightingale and many other woodland birds, if left alone, will have their young to rear when the caterpillar plague is at its worst. The robbing of a nest in May puts the birds back a fortnight, and when this second brood is out, the woodland trees and bushes are practically exempt from these pests. If you wander through any English wood during the first fortnight of June you can, in a few minutes, obtain hundreds of caterpillars, you cannot help seeing them, but if you search for them at the end of June you may look for hours without finding one. I have noticed the difference when waiting at nests of the nightingale. If the young are out during the first two weeks of

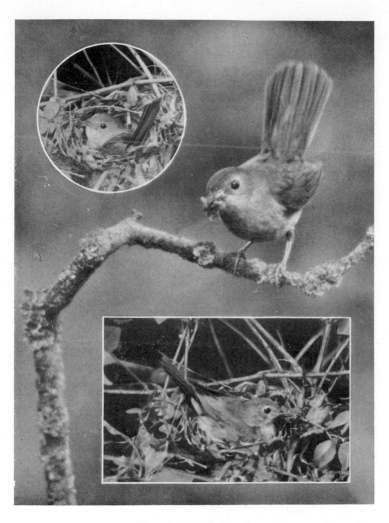

Female Nightingale
Inset top.—Sitting on eggs
Inset bottom.—Brooding over young

June the parents feed them entirely upon
caterpillars, and the visits to the nest are very
frequent, but it is a very different story when
the nest has young which must be fed during
the last fortnight of June. I have photographed
and watched nightingales under all conditions,
and at all times during the nesting season, and
I have always found that these late young do
not have anything like the quantity of food
given to them, because the parents find they
have to work very much harder and longer in
searching for it. The later food consists of
worms, if the weather is not too dry, large
flies, spiders and, in fact, any insects they can
find, but not the hairy caterpillars which make
their appearance at this time. The parents of
the late broods search for a lot of the food on
the ground, while the parents of earlier broods
find all the food they want on the bushes close
to the nest. One famous collector in writing
to another said that this statement of mine
was piffle, and it was waste of time to read such
nonsense ! To the collectors it may seem so,
but to those who really study nature, and see
the woods and fields at all seasons, it is found
that it is a very solid fact that cannot be
contradicted. If caterpillars are destroyed, say
in a garden, where just a few may be found,
it will mean that in time the gardener is quite
free of these pests, but if they are left alone

and not molested by enemies, he will find that the following year their numbers are increased, until they become a plague. Exactly the same thing applies to our woods and orchards, where the birds are the insect destroyers ; prevent those birds from rearing families at the critical time, by taking their first clutches of eggs when insect pests are at their worst, which is at the end of May and beginning of June, and the collector is doing his part in assisting in the destruction of our crops.

Many bird lovers have asked the question, How do young birds learn to sing ? It is certain that some of them do not hear their parents, for many of the latter do not sing after they leave the eggs. Young nightingales have plenty of opportunities for hearing their parent, for I have previously mentioned that the male sings right up to the time when they leave the nest. I have heard the nightingale going through a remarkable performance. This consisted of the male bird singing his wonderful song as he stood within a few inches of the nest, but the whole was given in such a subdued tone that it could not have been heard at a distance of more than three or four yards. I have often wondered whether he was giving his family a lesson, there is no other explanation I can offer.

If the parents are disturbed or worried

in any way during the period of feeding tho young in the nest, the latter are induced to leave before they are really ready. Many bird photographers, in their anxiety to obtain photographs, do not seem to study the birds themselves ; clumsy hides are built, the camera is placed too close to the nest, and the surroundings are cut away to such an extent that it is practically impossible, when their task is finished, to cover the nest over, to hide it from the numerous enemies which are always on the look-out for young birds. I have heard of numbers of instances of bird photographers causing rare birds to desert their eggs or young, simply because they did not know the habits of their subjects well enough to know how to go to work. When a photographer has finished with the nest, he should be able to replace the branches or other cover, so that anyone passing the spot would not know that any disturbance had taken place. Under careless conditions the parents will call their young from the nest before they can fly ; the result is that most of these youngsters come to an untimely end. If the nest is left undisturbed, the young will remain inside until they are able to fly with ease. Right up to the time of their young leaving the nest, nightingales keep strictly to their territory, but when the youngsters do commence to fly they wander at random over the wood, although from my own observations it seems that the parents do their best to keep them inside their domain; they get very excited if they begin to fly far, uttering their warning whistle "pui-pui" followed by the low "purr."

The young soon commence to find their own food; later in the summer both parents and young go to the elder bushes and devour the berries, for this is food which they are fond of; other edible berries are also eaten, such as wild raspberries. But with the ripening of our fruit the nightingales leave, and by the middle of September most have left the country to travel to Northern and Central Africa, where they spend our winter. In many woods the birds leave quite by the beginning of August, but whether these actually leave the country then I cannot say; some may move slowly south or south-east, picking up food on their way to the sea. The earliest record of one leaving the country was August 17th, when one was seen at Dungeness Lighthouse, and the latest October 1st, observed at Hanois Lighthouse in the Channel Islands.

It is not easy to put the nightingale's song into words; if half a dozen people attempted it, I doubt if two would use the same syllables. It is, however, easy to distinguish it from the song of other birds, for there is nothing like it

to be heard in the woods. On many occasions
I have been told that there was a nightingale
singing in a certain part, and when I have gone
to investigate it has been a thrush. The only
reason this bird's song is confused with that
of the nightingale is that it often sings late in
the summer time, sometimes when it is almost
dark, and many country dwellers think that
any bird which sings when all other song is
stilled must be a nightingale. For the same
reason the sedge-warbler, which is a clever
little mimic, is often mistaken for this woodland
songster.

A thrush repeats each bar of its song two,
three, or even four times ; put into words,
these bars sound like the words " pretty-dick,
pretty-dick, do-it-now, do-it-now, stick-to-it,
stick-to-it," etc., etc. The notes of the blackbird
are a deep contralto, and it is a rambling song
with no repetition of actual notes, although the
whole song is repeated at intervals of ten or
twenty seconds. The sedge-warbler's song is
harsh and jerky, but it can mimic other birds,
but I have never heard it attempt to repeat
the notes of the nightingale. Other woodland
birds with fine songs are the garden-warbler
and blackcap. The song of the former is a
continuous and lovely rich warble, continued
for ten or fifteen seconds ; that of the blackcap
is similar, but shorter in length and some of

itself in Scotland and other places where it is not found by placing its eggs in nests of robins, but although some of these attempts have been successful, as far as the rearing of the young was concerned, they have never returned to their birthplaces.

Garden-warbler at nest and sitting

The Garden-Warbler

Description.—Length, 5·5 inches. Upper parts, olive-brown; wings and tail, darker; rather inconspicuous paler line over eye; under parts, greyish-white; legs and feet, greyish-brown; eyes, brown.

Field Characters.—Can best be distinguished by its song, which is a continuous rich warble, quite one of the best songs to be heard in our woods. The song is given from the heart of some thick bramble bush or hedge, the singer is restless, constantly making short journeys, but seldom showing itself. When seen, the olive-brown back and greyish-white breast help us to distinguish it from the whitethroats; also it appears to be rounder or more plump than the more slender whitethroat. Found in gardens, especially where there are many old gooseberry bushes, woods, coppices and small meadows with untrimmed hedges around.

NEXT to the nightingale the garden-warbler is my favourite woodland bird; its wonderful song, which I prefer to that of the blackcap, is always entrancing and delightful to listen to. It is also one of the first birds I knew as a child. On a large market-garden where I spent the first happy years of my life there were thousands of gooseberry bushes, and I often saw the confiding small warbler sitting on her fragile nest, and on many occasions I parted the branches and actually touched the bird as she covered her eggs or young.

We hear the garden-warbler singing in all

parts of the wood, but if a preference for any spot is shown it is the outskirts rather than the interior ; a low uncut hedge running alongside a wood with plenty of bramble at its base will be an ideal nesting site. In our nightingale wood there is a hedge of this description about five hundred yards in length, and in this, or in the bushes just inside the wood, we find most of the nests.

It has often been stated that in districts where we find the garden-warbler the blackcap is absent, and vice versa; but my experience is just the opposite, and I have found blackcaps and garden-warblers nesting in close proximity. I have noticed, however, that when the garden-warbler is in full song the blackcaps in the immediate vicinity are silent, while if the blackcaps are singing, the garden-warblers are not heard : this rather curious fact may account for many of the statements that the birds are not found together.

The garden-warbler is one of the latest warblers to arrive in this country ; it winters in Africa, arriving in our district about the last week of April. The males arrive a week or ten days before the females, and during that period sing lustily throughout the day.

Careful observation will show that practically every British breeding bird has a territory of its own during the nesting season ; with some of the small birds, such as the warblers, these territories are small, and are also governed by the number of males in the district. For instance, in places where there are few garden warblers a pair might have a territory covering a square quarter of a mile, while in districts where the birds are more crowded the territory covers a tract about two hundred yards each way. The larger birds, such as buzzards, ravens and eagles, have their territories, but they cover vast tracts of country. Rooks are birds which keep carefully inside their well-marked domains. If we watch the birds at any rookery during the period of feeding the young, we will see the parents go off to certain feeding grounds, and day after day they use these. In stormy weather, when the wind is against them, the birds will often have difficulty in getting home with a heavy supply of food, and I have often wondered why they do not change their district to fly against the wind when unladen, and with it when heavily loaded, but they do not do so.

The loud song given out by the male garden-warblers immediately after their arrival is undoubtedly for two reasons, the first to tell their neighbours that they have taken possession of their territory, and the second to attract a female. Migration takes a vast toll of the warblers each season ; it is surprising

47

that so many do manage to get through the perilous journey of thousands of miles each spring and autumn. In this changeable climate of ours we do sometimes have it favourable for both male and female birds on their journey; but it does happen, and more often than is generally supposed, that after the male of one species arrives, the females are driven out of their course by strong winds, or perish while crossing the sea. Those lighthouses which are not fitted with perches around the light are a source of great danger, for the birds dash into the glass and are killed. Ten years ago I saw a heap of garden-warblers which had perished in this way by striking the glass of one of our southern lighthouses.

In the spring of 1929 the majority of male garden-warblers came safely through their journey, but thousands of females must have met with a mishap, for there were whole districts in many parts of England where no females arrived. One district was the southern parts of Sussex, and another the counties of Bedfordshire and Berkshire. Each season we have garden-warblers in our garden, and the usual custom is for the male to sing loudly before the female arrives, and lessen his singing after she settles down, while little song is heard after the end of June. In 1929, however, there were no females in the district, and the

48

result was that our male sang incessantly
right through May, June, July and August ; he
did not lessen his efforts or give up hope of
attracting a female until the middle of August,
and even after that we occasionally heard
short bursts of his song. It was a most
delightful exhibition of avian music, and often
while a tennis party was in progress the male
would sing continuously the whole afternoon
within a few yards of the players. But his
efforts were all in vain, for no female arrived
to assist him in bringing up a family.

During this period of waiting and singing
he built several dummy nests. All those built
by the garden-warbler, for the male will make
them even when he has a mate sitting on eggs,
are very flimsy affairs, just a few fine dried
grasses placed cross-wise on a spraying branch
are sufficient ; each dummy looks like the
foundations of the proper nest, some have
enough grass to support the bird, while others
consist of half a dozen strands. But during
the season when no mate arrived he seemed
to take more care in making these dummies,
perhaps thinking that these, in addition to his
song, might attract a female to his domain !

When the song of the male has attracted
a female to his territory his next efforts are
spent in courting her. His display is at times
quite attractive, for he will fly up short distances,

then with vibrating wings and spread tail slowly descend to the branch on which she is perched ; he will then open and raise his wings above his back, raise and lower his tail, meanwhile uttering low twitterings, something like a very much subdued edition of his song. Occasionally he will pick up a small piece of leaf, or more likely a piece of grass, and holding this before her, he again goes through the display with his wings, as though he was telling her that it was time she commenced to build the nest.

Most of the actual nest-building is done by the female. He will collect grasses and carry them to the site, afterwards standing by and singing while she works. The nest construction usually takes place in the early morning ; most birds, in fact, seem to prefer to build in the first part of the day, and it is finished in about five days. Although rather a flimsy structure, and not too carefully fastened to its supports, I have never known one break away, as often happens with the nest of the blackcap.

If the garden-warbler arrives early in his territory, say during the third week of April, and the hen joins him a week later, nest-building is not commenced correspondingly early. I have not known the nest to be built before the middle of May; usually in this district it

is late, the last week of May, or first of June
being preferred. In the wood which I mention
in my chapter on the nightingale, and in other
woods in the district, we have usually found
the garden-warbler sitting on fresh eggs at
the commencement of the last week of June;
but these may have been second attempts at
nest-building, for if this warbler builds earlier,
when the leaves on the hedges are small, the
nest is more easily seen, and is robbed by the
numerous enemies to be found in the woods.
One brood only is reared, as is usual with
most birds which are not resident in the
country.

The eggs usually have a ground colour of
yellowish - white, blotched and spotted with
large and small markings of olive and brown,
the surface being glossy, altogether rather
handsome little eggs. The nest is often built
on an overhanging branch of the hawthorn,
also in the tangled undergrowth at the base
of the hedges ; a gooseberry bush is also
a favourite site ; I have found many in
this latter situation. The male assists with
incubation ; he will approach the nest singing
loudly, perhaps to show his mate that he is
willing to take his turn, for she replies with a
few low notes, to afterwards stand on the edge
of the nest fluttering her wings, while he slips
over the eggs to take her place ; the same

pretty scene is repeated when she returns a couple of hours or so later.

Incubation lasts thirteen days. When the young first leave the eggs they are blind, their eyes opening on the third day; then they grow quickly, to leave their home in about a fortnight. Both parents are kept busy during the period the young are in the nest, and also after they leave, for they can devour large quantities of insects. The food brought to the nest varies according to the time the young arrive. If the birds nest fairly early, and they succeed in having young to rear during the first fortnight of June, the food consists principally of green caterpillars; but the later broods have many winged insects given to them. I have on several occasions watched the parents feeding the young in the nest during the first week of July, when the latter were about three days old, and I have seen very few caterpillars brought to them, but many moths, large flies, and other insects which I was not able to distinguish.

The young are fed by both parents during the first four days after leaving the eggs. The female spends a good part of the day in brooding over them, while the male brings food to the nest. On these visits she will sometimes slip off and allow him to feed, while at other times he hands the food to her, which she takes with many happy flutterings of her wings, and afterwards passes on to the young.

During the whole period of feeding the young, both before and after they leave the nest, the parents are always on the look-out for enemies; on the slightest sign of danger both utter a loud alarm note, "teck, teck," and so persistent are they that most of the other birds in the immediate vicinity fly to the spot and join in the chorus of alarms. While I was waiting in my hide at one nest a grey squirrel approached within about twenty yards, and for ten minutes the excitement was great, for blackbirds, thrushes, whitethroats, nightingales, and wrens fluttered around, each uttering its own note of alarm. One wild bird takes very little notice of another's song, but let that same bird give out one danger signal, and every bird within hearing recognizes it and is instantly on the alert. The foxes, badgers and other mammals found in the woods are able to interpret every note of alarm. I have watched the badger working diligently with his nose in the grass, searching for worms and leather-jackets, food of which he is very fond, but on the startled cry of a blackbird reaching him, he has disappeared so cleverly, that it looked almost as though he had vanished into air!

At a nest which I found in a gooseberry bush the female was accidentally killed during the period of feeding. The young were about six days old when this tragedy occurred, and I visited the nest daily to see if the male would carry on. Examination of the female showed that there was a small wound in the neck, which looked as if she had flown against one of the sharp thorns on the bush, and when I found her she was lying dead by the side of the nest. I was pleased to see that the male continued to feed his family, and they eventually left the nest in his charge. It was interesting to note that after the loss of his mate he sang loudly when I approached the nest. It is rather unusual for the male to sing after the young leave their eggs, and I wondered if he had commenced again, to attract another mate. I have known several instances of male birds carrying on with the duties of feeding the young after losing their mates. A male blackbird with a family of five to look after continued to feed them after a cat had killed the female, but directly the young were able to fly he mated up again, and another nest was built close to the old one.

The young garden - warblers remain with their parents for several weeks after leaving the nest. If we approach the family as they are searching for food both parents become very excited, uttering their harsh alarm note, "teck-teck." The parents show their young

54

how to capture insect food, also leading them to the elder bushes, where quantities of the black berries are devoured.

It is not easy to describe the song, but when we hear a continued and beautiful warble full of rich loud notes we may be sure it is the garden-warbler singing. The song of the black-cap is similar, but we can distinguish one from the other because the blackcap sings in short bursts, while the garden-warbler will continue for half a minute at a time. A really good singing blackcap has more variety in its song, and the actual notes are richer, but if we hear the song continued for even fifteen seconds it is almost certain to be that of the garden-warbler.

The Blackcap

Description.—Length, 5·5 inches. Upper parts, ashy-brown; head, glossy-black; under parts, ashy-grey, lighter on chin; bill, brown; eyes, hazel. Adult female has a reddish-brown head and whole body slightly browner.

Field Characters.—Male can be distinguished by the jet-black crown, and female by the reddish-brown crown. At first glance the male might be confused with the willow tit or marsh tit, but larger size and brilliant song distinguish it. Found in woods, gardens containing bushes, especially rhododendrons, coppices and lanes with untrimmed hedges. Song, a loud, rich warble, intermixed with many imitations of notes of other woodland birds.

THE blackcap arrives in this country from Africa and southern Europe earlier than the garden-warbler. I have known the blackcap to be sitting on a clutch of eggs a week before the garden-warbler was heard. The earliest record is 10th March. These early arrivals are probably those which winter in Europe. The main body of migrants come into this country from the second week of April to the end of that month, but a few later arrivals straggle on to the second week of May.

The outskirts of woods and the bushes bordering garden paths seem to be preferred by this small bird; we seldom find it right in the heart of the wood. Every nest I have

57

found of the blackcap has been within a few feet of a woodland drive or garden path.

Those blackcaps which arrive in this country during March will often have difficulty in finding enough food, and they also seem to suffer from the cold, for they take advantage of every little burst of sunshine, and we will see them on frosty mornings sitting on a twig of a sheltered bush, where the beams from the rising sun shine upon them, their feathers are puffed out and sometimes the wings raised so to allow every bit of warmth to penetrate to their bodies. If a fly or some other insect should show itself it is instantly pounced upon, and the fortunate one to obtain it goes back to its perch to continue its warmth-giving exercise.

The blackcap is quite one of the most interesting of our warblers, owing to the rather remarkable display it gives while courting. On its arrival in this country it gives out its best song—rich, loud notes of great purity, and we find that in the birds' territory there is usually a favourite perch from which it sings. The song is not so prolonged as that of the garden-warbler, some of the outbursts are very short, lasting six or eight seconds or so. This early song is probably given first to proclaim its territory, and secondly to attract a female. A few days after the latter arrive the greatest excitement is shown by the males. If two happen to court the same female in a tract of woodland which has already been appropriated by one, the owner will do his best to drive the trespasser away. They will fall to the ground, pecking and tearing at each other, now and again both combatants pausing for breath, with their breasts heaving and their beaks wide open. The female appears to take very little interest in these fights, but when the owner of the territory succeeds in driving his opponent away, and he usually does manage this, for he is so determined, he seems to lose himself in his excitement. Instead of uttering his own song, which contains notes of such wonderful purity, he will bring in imitations of other bird notes, raise the pitch of this mixed song, and do all he can to show the bird he wishes to win that there is great variety in his music.

But it is in his courting display that the blackcap is so attractive ; he puts his small body into some remarkable poses, puffing out the feathers of his head, breast and back, while the tail is spread out like a wide-open fan, and raised and lowered at right angles to the body ; sometimes he will be facing the female, at other times his back or side is turned to her, and during this performance he will occasionally utter a few wild notes which do not seem to belong to his song, or the song of any other bird ! Occasionally, during this performance, the male which he was supposed to have defeated will show himself again, and both birds will fly up into the air with wings fluttering and beaks working at each other. This courting display may continue for three or four days, while at other times a very short courtship takes place, for the female is very erratic in her ways, sometimes accepting her lover at once, and at other times keeping him in suspense.

The nest is built inside a bush or in the thick undergrowth near its base ; that of the garden-warbler is more often on the outside of a bush ; most of the nests of the blackcap that I have found have been well inside, and at heights from the ground varying from three to just over six feet. The female does the chief part of the building, although the male will do his part if he happens to arrive at the partly-built home with material while his mate is absent. The materials used are fine dry grasses, bents and roots, with occasionally a little horsehair as a lining. It is a fragile structure, and some that I have seen have been badly fastened to their supports, and when discovered were tipping over, and if it had not been for my attention in fixing them up securely the young must have fallen out.

Blackcap. Male at nest and sitting on eggs

My experience is that the male blackcap performs the chief part of incubation during the hours of daylight. Many of the nests that I have watched in gardens and small coppices have shown that from early morning to sometimes well over mid-day the male has been upon the eggs. And again, while feeding the young, the male makes about three visits to the nest to one by the female.

Numbers of bird-lovers have recorded their experiences while watching our wild birds at their nests, but on a great many occasions they have not been too well concealed, and the birds have known of their presence. I always think that this gives a false impression of the home-life of our birds. If watching is to be accurate it should be done from a well-built hide, and the birds themselves should be quite unconscious that a human being is near. By using a periscope, instead of a peep-hole, a hide can be completely covered with branches or other cover, while the observer inside has a perfectly open view of everything that is going on outside. When many of our warblers know they are being watched the male will behave in a curious manner. The female, having more parental instinct, will be the first to take food to the nest, and when she has fed the young once or twice, and finds that there is no danger, she will afterwards behave in an almost normal

61

manner. The male, however, will hop around the nest, keeping in the background as much as possible, and every time his mate arrives with food he will fuss around and much closer to the nest, as though he was waiting his turn; but directly she goes off, and is well out of sight, he slinks to the background once more. It looks almost as though he intended to show her how well he was doing his duty while she was near, but not having enough pluck to actually go to the nest after her departure! In the case of the blackcap this performance is reversed, and it is the male which does the feeding, while the female is slinking among the leaves.

Near some of the nests that I have found there has been a dummy nest made by the male, but not two or three as we find with the garden-warbler. One nest containing eggs was built in a small bush on the banks of a brook on the margin of a wood; on the opposite side of the water there stood a small elder bush, and in this the male blackcap built his dummy. It was constructed more solidly than the dummies made by his near relation the garden-warbler. One day, while I was approaching their haunt, I heard the male singing lustily from the elder bush. I stalked up as silently as I could. I reached the bush and he still continued to sing. Very carefully and slowly

I parted the branches and looked down upon a delightful little scene : there was the male blackcap busy on his nest, he appeared to be entangled with a long grass stem, which was twisted over his body, but notwithstanding this, he turned round and round in the rough structure, pressing his breast against the materials, and so shaping the interior ; but what made it so interesting was that he was so taken up with his work, and so pleased with himself, that he sang loudly the whole time, and failed to see the human observer. But suddenly he looked up, saw me, and flew on, and as far as I could determine he never returned to this dummy to make any additions to it.

We usually find the young in the nest about the end of May, but I have known a bird to have its full clutch of five eggs on 25th April. The eggs are rather beautiful, varying greatly in the ground colour and markings. The majority have a light stone or buff ground colour, covered with blotches and spots of brown and grey ; some are a delicate pink with pinkish-brown markings, while there are many other varieties ; most are very like those of the garden-warbler, but if anything smaller and less glossy.

Incubation lasts fourteen days, and for the first four days after the young leave both parents spend a deal of time in brooding over them; the male seems to brood more than his mate during the day. If the young arrive during May they are fed chiefly upon caterpillars collected close to the nest; like all young birds they are capable of devouring large quantities, always being ready for the food brought to them.

If an enemy approaches the nest while it contains eggs or young, a loud alarm note, "tac-tac-tac," is uttered, which has the effect of attracting other birds. At one nest which I was photographing a stoat began nosing around at the base of the bush; it seemed almost as if it must scent the young in the nest above, and the parents became wildly excited; but suddenly it left, came directly towards my hide, crept inside under the canvas covering and smelt my boot! Without a moment's hesitation it turned and bolted full speed from the spot, much to the relief of both the birds and the photographer! Directly it had gone the male blackcap returned to the nest to continue looking after his family.

The young remain with their parents for several weeks after they leave the nest, and at this time we seldom hear the male sing his loud spring song, but we do hear a subdued edition of it; this is continued right on to the autumn, and now and again we are fortunate to be near enough to see the singer. It is really a low warble through which we can distinguish a few of the summer notes, a contented little song, as though he was singing to please himself instead of holding forth to attract a mate. Many of our warblers have this autumn song, but it is so little known because we must be within a few feet of the singers to hear it. The chiff-chaff and willow-warbler sing on their passage south in August and September, but neither song has the vivacity connected with the spring efforts.

The Whitethroat

Description.—Length, 5·5 inches. Upper parts, warm brown ; wings and tail, slightly darker ; the outer pair of tail feathers, white ; the next pair tipped with white ; under parts, white, but chin and throat a purer white, and latter tinged with pale pink, the pink being more pronounced immediately after their arrival, or after a few days' rain ; in dry weather the pink becomes dulled with dirt or dust ; bill, dark-brown ; legs and feet, pale brown ; eyes, yellowish-brown.

Field Characters.—The most prominent habit of this bird, and the easiest way of distinguishing it from other warblers is its method of throwing itself into the air above the hedges, then dropping like a tangled heap of feathers back to cover, meanwhile uttering its loud, snatchy song. The latter is a jumble of notes given in snatches, either from the depth of the hedgerow, and more frequently from large patches of cow-parsley or nettles, or in the air as described.

THE whitethroat winters in Africa, coming to this country in April or even early March, but the majority arrive about the third week of April. The male very soon announces its arrival by uttering its snatchy song, given with great gusto. The old haunts seem to be used season after season, and it is more than probable that the same pairs, if they survive the perils of migration, nest in the same territories for several years in succession. The males arrive about a week before the females; but if we go near the male

67

bird before a mate arrives he will scold us most vehemently, and with raised crest he utters a harsh "churr, churr," a note which evidently means anger, often followed by his note of alarm, "teck-teck."

The territory occupied by a pair of white-throats is usually small; those which I have had under observation in our garden occupy a domain a third the size of that covered by our pair of garden-warblers. The garden itself, which is about one acre in extent, offers excellent cover for our warblers, and we have two pairs of whitethroats, one appearing to keep to the side bordering the north-west, and the other pair on the south-east. When the females arrive, and occasionally before, the males fight, but these contests are rather feeble affairs compared with those of some other small birds. There is a lot of bluff and show, but little damage ; the two males will attack each other with beaks and fluttering wings, continue for a few seconds, then one, apparently thinking he is going to be defeated, breaks away and commences to search for food or preen his feathers. I have seen many birds commence the latter exercise during or after a fight, and it seems to me that it is a cunning little habit to cover cowardice ; however, both white-throats will do it, then one will make another feeble attack, and again in a minute or so they appear to be good friends. Now and again one will fly upwards, ten or twenty feet above the hedge, singing lustily, to drop in what looks like an untidy loose condition back to cover.

The courting display of the whitethroat is attractive because he puts such a lot of energy into it, seeming at times as if he was almost mad with delight. He will approach the female with lowered head and fluttering wings, then if she is on an open branch he throws himself into the air, erects his crest, spreads his tail, and flutters his wings so energetically that his downward flight seems almost to be out of control ; but before he actually drops on to the hen he recovers himself in rather a miraculous manner and settles by her side. On these upward and downward flights he sings loudly, these notes changing to low, soft ones as he once more flutters his wings while on the branch.

During the period of courtship, and sometimes even before the hen arrives in his territory, he will commence to build dummy nests ; but when she is constructing the nest which she intends to use he will also make one, often to be followed by another while she is sitting. These dummy nests of the whitethroat are very different to those clumsy efforts of most of the other warblers, for this bird makes a nest every bit as good as that used by the hen for

69

her eggs. I have seen it stated that the cock alone builds the nest used by the hen for eggs, the latter adding only a few tufts of down as lining ; but this must be an error of observation, or other whitethroats behave differently to the many I have watched. I find that the hen builds the nest, or the chief part of it, the male assisting in bringing materials. Nest-building is rather a lengthy affair. I have known birds to be at work for ten days before it was ready for eggs.

The site chosen for the nest varies. A common position is among nettles or hedge parsley near the base of a hedgerow, or on grassy banks covered with these plants ; small bushes standing alone beneath a hedge, and small clumps of bramble in a similar position are often occupied. The nest is well built, strong and fixed securely to its supports ; the materials are fine dry grasses and roots ; it is well lined with hair, and has several bits of down or wool dotted about inside.

When the hen is sitting the male will make a demonstration around one of his dummy nests, and this looks very much as though he was attracting us to that spot to draw us from the nest occupied by his mate. I have watched this clever performance on many occasions and shown it to my friends. As we approach the haunt the male becomes excited over his

Female Whitethroat which fell exhausted over her nest

Inset.—Female with food for young

nest, constantly dropping into the cover close
to it, and uttering his alarm notes; then as
we get nearer he actually tries to show us where
the nest is concealed by fluttering from it.
I have mentioned this interesting incident
before in another book, and a well-known
critic has doubted it, even going so far as to
say that it is fictitious ! It is evident that
my critic has never seen this performance, but
that is no reason why it does not take place;
if he cares to make an appointment with me
almost any time during the last three weeks
of May I could show it him in our garden,
and convince him that the male whitethroat
does perform this cunning ruse to attract
supposed enemies from the nest occupied by
his mate.

The number of eggs laid is usually four or
five. The common type has a greenish ground
colour, speckled with fine lead-coloured spots,
with a darker zone around the large end;
other types have a stone ground colour, with
larger blotches instead of fine spots, and much
resemble the eggs of the lesser whitethroat.
Incubation lasts thirteen days, chiefly by the
hen, although the male will take his turn for
short periods each day while the hen goes off
to feed.

When feeding time comes the male does
equal work with his mate. For the first four

71

days after the young leave the eggs one of the parents remains to brood over them, while the other searches for food. After this both male and female work hard to satisfy the wants of their family. On three occasions I have seen the female return to the nest in an exhausted condition. She has given the food she has brought to the young, then fallen upon them, and with spread wings, drooping head, with beak open, she has slowly subsided until she almost fell off the nest. In one instance her eyes closed, her head fell over the side, and I thought she was just on the point of dying; but she appeared to pull herself together, and after a short rest of about five minutes she stood up on the approach of her mate and flew off to continue her work.

I obtained a cinema film of this scene, and it was included in one of my wild-bird films which have been shown in all parts of the world. At one performance, where I was not present to defend myself, a very great naturalist, sometime of the British Museum, actually stated that before the photograph was taken I had either drugged or injured the bird, and that it was not natural behaviour! This was a startling statement to make, and it shows how dangerous it is for a museum naturalist to criticize the work of a field naturalist. If I had never seen this exhausted

72

condition of the whitethroat in real life I might have thought the same, but I should not have made such a damaging statement without being sure of my facts. I have seen similar incidents with the reed-bunting and hedge-sparrow, and in each case it looked as though the bird was going to expire with exhaustion. This behaviour usually takes place during the early afternoon, for it is then that the hard-worked parents are beginning to feel tired after many hours of feeding. The afternoon and evening are not good times for photography at the nest, for I find that after three o'clock many birds rest from their labours, allowing the young to sleep if they are well - grown, or brooding over them and giving very little food if quite small.

The female whitethroat will often endeavour to attract us from her nest when it contains young : she will tumble from the nest to the ground, then with fluttering wings and spread tail drag herself along the ground. If we follow she will always keep just out of our reach, to fly up when she has succeeded in drawing us fifty yards or so from her young. I have followed many of these persevering birds. One which had her nest close to my garden gate did it every time I approached her, but quite the most interesting incident of this kind occurred in France during the war. A small bush stood by the side of a trench, and in this a whitethroat had her nest. The sound of bursting shells and the general disturbance all around were not sufficient to drive her from her old haunt, and she managed to bring up her family. When we went near enough to be, as she supposed, dangerous, she would tumble to the bottom of the trench, then feigning a broken wing or other damage, she dragged herself along, leading us, up the trench for about fifty yards, and always when she reached a certain spot, close to another small bush, she would fly up, settle on a twig, and with raised crest utter her alarm or other notes, seeming as if she was proud of having attracted us so far from her young.

I have never known the whitethroat, or in fact any migratory warbler, to have two broods. In some books on bird-life the authors state that this bird is double-brooded, but if it is I have been unfortunate, for I have not even heard of an instance. If the birds lose their family when they are quite small, say during the first day or two after leaving their eggs, then they will build another nest to endeavour to rear a family; but when they do succeed in bringing up their young so that they fly from the nest I doubt if they ever attempt to rear a second brood.

Willow-warblers

The Willow-Warbler

Description.—Length, 5 inches. Upper parts, olive-green inclining to yellow on the rump; wings and tail, brown; under parts, yellowish-white; bill, brown; eyes, hazel; legs and feet, pale brown.

Field characters.—Can best be distinguished by its song, which is a sweet warble, commences on a high note, then descends slightly, the notes being uttered quickly, then as they reach the lower tone seem to melt away. In general appearance like the chiffchaff and wood-warbler, can be distinguished from former by its legs, which are brown, while those of the chiffchaff are nearly black. The wood-warbler is rather larger and has a sulphur-yellow throat. The song of the chiffchaff is like its name, "chiff-chaff, chiffy-chaff," repeated many times in succession, while that of the wood-warbler often commences with a short whistle followed by "sip, sip, sip, tr-r-r-r-r-r-ree-e-e. All three songs are quite distinct.

In the spring and summer months the willow-warbler is one of the commonest if not the most common bird in the British Islands. The only bird to compete with it for this honour is the meadow-pipit. The latter is common on all the large, open spaces, such as the moors of Wales and Scotland; in other suitable places there are such vast tracts where we find this bird that it is not too easy to compare its status with that of the willow-warbler. But there are large portions of the country where it is not found, while the willow-warbler is to be heard

75

singing in almost every little tract of woodland, road-side coppices, wooded gardens and fields with trees alongside the hedges, from Cornwall in the south to mid-Scotland in the north. I have heard it singing in a little group of trees on the wild Cairngorm mountains, and these marked the last belt of trees on their steep sides, yet there in that lonely spot several pairs were singing merrily.

The willow - warbler is one of the first warblers to arrive in this country, the earliest record being 9th March. We often hear a few singing in the southern counties during the last week of March, but the main body of migrants arrive about the second week of April, and directly on arrival announce that they have come, by repeatedly uttering their merry little song.

I am always surprised to note the sleek appearance of this diminutive bird directly after its arrival. We always have not less than two pairs in our garden, so I have good opportunities of watching them. I remember one male which I saw in the garden in the fairly early morning. It must have settled down in its old haunt during the night, and although it had completed a journey of probably two or three thousand miles, there did not appear to be a feather out of place. The most interesting feature about this particular arrival was the fact that the male was singing from the same little bush that a willow-warbler's nest was under the previous summer. Was he the owner of that nest, and had he settled there to see if the site was suitable for nesting operations on this return visit ?

The territory occupied by a pair of willow-warblers is very much smaller than that of the garden-warbler. The reason may be that the former bird is very much more common, and suitable breeding territories would be more difficult to hold against rivals if they were large. A tract of woodland twenty or thirty yards square will be quite sufficient for a [pair of willow-warblers to settle in. I know some woods where practically every tract of about this size is occupied by a pair.

On his arrival in his domain the male sings incessantly all through the day. When you first hear the song it appears to be very pleasing, but when you hear it at half-minute intervals just outside your study window for hours in succession it becomes very monotonous. Each male does not intend to risk calling a mate to his territory by lack of song. The females will sometimes appear two or three days after the males, but usually a week passes before they put in an appearance. During this period the males appear to try to out-sing each other, and desperate fights take place. Although the willow-warbler is small, it is a most determined fighter if a rival enters his domain. I have never known these fights to end fatally, but I have seen the vanquished so badly knocked about that it looked doubtful if he would recover. The birds fight on the branches, on the ground, and even in the air while one is gaining the advantage in driving his opponent away. During these encounters the birds are as a rule silent, but occasionally we hear an angry note uttered when one gets a particularly hard blow home.

On the arrival of the females the males make rather a feeble display. They are slow in their actions, and will stand with wings spread and lowered by the side of their bodies for half a minute at a time; while the hen, if she approves of these advances, will give a similar display and utter low, pleasing notes meanwhile; the expanded wings are vibrated with a pretty quivering action. The male whinchat will vibrate his wings in a similar manner when showing off before his mate. I once succeeded in photographing this action; the exposure was one three-hundreth part of a second. It will give some idea of the speed of this vibration when I mention that in the finished photographs the wing-tips were slightly blurred, showing that this exposure was not

78

rapid enough to obtain a true record of the movement.

The males will fight again during courtship if females are scarce in their district. In our garden the sexes appear to be evenly balanced, for both pairs soon settle down to nest building. Very little time is wasted after the birds are paired, and nest building commences almost at once. The construction of the nest takes about a week, the female doing most of the actual building, but between his bursts of song I have seen the male assist her by carrying material. The nest is very cleverly concealed among the grass on the ground. It is so cunningly worked into the surroundings that from above it is almost impossible to tell that the birds have been building at that spot, for the nest is domed over with a small entrance at the side. Some of the nests that I have found have had a feather placed over the entrance, so that when the birds entered or left their nest, they had to push past it, and it sprang back into position like a small, self-closing door.

Incubation lasts thirteen days. Those competent to judge say that it is performed by the hen only. This is probably correct, for there seems practically no period during the day when we do not hear the male singing ; if he spent several hours upon the eggs his song would not be heard. He does, however, look after his sitting mate, and many times during the day carries down a tit-bit for her. When the young arrive he is a hard worker and does his duty well. For the first four days the hen spends a lot of her time in brooding over the young, while the male brings food to the nest at half-minute intervals if caterpillars are common around, and at the time when the young appear there is usually a vast supply close at hand.

At one nest I watched and photographed rather a pretty scene. The hen had been brooding on her young for at least two hours, and during all that time had not taken any food herself, handing all that the male brought to the young or allowing him to give it to them. On his next visit he brought a nice plump caterpillar about one inch in length, and he evidently meant it for her. When he reached the nest he stood outside and called her. She left her young to make way for him, but he refused to enter the nest, and instead held the food close to her beak, uttered a few low, pleasing notes and vibrated his wings. I knew that she must be hungry and this special beakful of food must have been very tempting; but although she responded with notes and wing vibrations she would not take it, but showed every sign that he should give it to the young. Again he held it close to her beak, and at last she took it from him, began to swallow it herself, but thought better of it, changed her mind, passed into the nest, and handed it to one of the young, which all the time had had their necks raised and beaks wide open. After the food had been disposed of she went back to her duties of brooding over them.

Those who have studied wild nature will have discovered that there is very little sympathy shown by one species to another, or by parents to their young. If a youngster falls out of the nest before it is fledged the parents will take no notice of it. Glaring instances of this are seen when the young cuckoo ejects its nest companions. I have seen young meadow-pipits, hedge-sparrows and sedge-warblers lying practically on the edge of the nest, and although when the parents arrive with food these have raised their heads and opened their beaks, the old birds have ignored them, giving all the food to the young cuckoo inside the nest. But I have come across a few instances of one species appearing to take compassion on another. While photographing with my cinema camera the home life at the nest of a song-thrush I was surprised to see a grey wagtail pause in its flight and hand the food in her beak to the young thrushes. The nest of the wagtail was about one hundred feet away, but in her flight to her young she happened to pass over this nest, saw the open beaks and, seemingly, could not resist them. Another interesting instance took place while I was photographing a pair of willow-warblers feeding their young. The latter were outside their nest, sitting on a twig near, and I was able to expose several plates upon them. While waiting I heard a slight noise on the edge of my hide, and turning my eyes, I saw a wren pushing its way through a peephole. This inquisitive little bird came right inside, settled on my camera, examined this with its bright eyes, then went back the way it came, and to my intense surprise flew straight on to the branch on which my baby willow-warblers were sitting. It looked at them for a moment or so, just giving me time to expose a plate on this interesting scene ; then it flew off, to return in less than a minute with what looked like a small insect in its beak, which it actually offered to one of the young willow-warblers. Other bird photographers have come across many instances of a strange bird visiting and feeding the young in the nest they were watching, but this is the only instance, apart from that of the young cuckoo, where I have known it to occur outside the nest. It looks very much as though some birds cannot resist the sight of an open beak. The young cuckoo certainly has some remarkable influence over other parent birds, for it is quite a common occurrence to see several species attending to its wants after it leaves the nest. I have known five different species to feed a young cuckoo which was reared in the first place by a pair of hedge-sparrows ; but the most remarkable instance that ever came under my notice, was observed by two Scottish naturalists, who actually saw fourteen meadow - pipits in attendance upon one young cuckoo !

But to return to the willow-warbler. There is one curious habit the bird has, and that is the frequency with which a pair will desert their nest for no apparent reason. After the hen has been sitting on her full clutch of eggs for two or three days she will suddenly leave them and commence to build another nest close by. In our garden this desertion frequently takes place. This spring (1932) three nests were built by one pair. The first was deserted before eggs were laid in it, and a second was built on the opposite side of the tennis court on a bank in the meadow just outside. The full clutch of eggs was laid in this, and although it had not been disturbed in any way, the hen left it, to construct her third nest on a bank in the garden. All three nests were within thirty yards of one another, and all in equally safe positions.

The number of eggs laid is usually six or seven ; they are white, covered with fine light - red or reddish - brown spots. Seven youngsters is a large family for such small birds, and their efforts are greatly taxed when the young are ready to leave. I have seen them come to the nest near which I was hiding four times in a minute, and although this speed was not kept up all the time, the average for three hours worked out at two visits every minute. This gives us some idea of the vast amount of good these insect-feeding birds do. Each pair, and as I have previously mentioned they are spread all over the country, will during the ten or twelve days in which the young remain in the nest account for at least ten thousand insects, chiefly caterpillars, and even after the young leave, they keep up the same hard work in feeding them. I know few prettier sights than a family of young willow-warblers sitting on a branch outside the nest ; they look so plump and well fed and wait so contentedly, then when a parent arrives with food, all open their beaks hoping it will be their turn, to settle down for another short wait until the parents pay another visit.

There is a very great mortality among young birds after they leave their nests, and especially with the young willow-warblers ; they appear to sit in such prominent positions and numbers must be captured by the numerous enemies always on the look-out for food. Jays

84

and magpies will snap up many, while grey squirrels, which are becoming so common in our woods, will account for some just after they leave the nest. The arrival of a red or grey squirrel in a territory occupied by a willow-warbler will cause a lot of excitement in the wood, for the persistent alarm note of this small bird, which is a short, sharp whistle " pui, pui," will bring many other birds to the spot.

When the young begin to fly, they wander at random over the wood followed by their parents, and the well-marked boundaries over which the latter seldom wandered are forgotten. The song at this time ceases, but we hear it again at the end of July and in the early autumn while the birds are commencing their long southern journey. Day after day in September we hear the song of willow-warblers in our garden, but these are not from the birds which have spent the summer with us, they have already departed ; these intermittent songs are from travellers passing over, now and again uttering their song as they move on. The song lacks the vivacity of the spring songs, for in September it is quite a mournful little ditty.

The Sedge-Warbler

Description.—Length, 4·75 inches. Upper parts, reddish-brown; tawny on lower part and tail. Under parts : chin and throat, white; remainder, buff; legs and feet, pale greyish-brown; eyes, brown. A broad yellow stripe over eye.

Field characters.—Usually found near water or marshy ground, but often in places a good distance from water, where the undergrowth is thick. The song is harsh, consisting of a jumble of notes, with very little music in them, with the notes of other birds intermixed, the song of the swallow, the call note of the chaffinch, whitethroat and blackbird are often introduced. Sings by day and night. The rather rich colouring and broad eye-stripe help to distinguish it from other warblers.

THE sedge-warbler winters in Africa and Asia Minor. It arrives here about the third week of April, and like most of our warblers announces its arrival by song very soon afterwards. My experience with this warbler has been chiefly on the banks of the Tring reservoirs, which are such a paradise for our small birds. It is quite the commonest bird to be found there. On warm spring nights there is a chorus of song from these birds, with the slightly less harsh song of the reed-warblers filling up the gaps. As the birds are so numerous the territories occupied by each pair are necessarily small, but

87

I find that this bird is always content with a very small tract of country. We have a pair in our garden each spring. The nearest water is a very fine public swimming pool about one hundred yards away, but the birds remain in a short stretch of hedgerow during the period of nesting.

The sedge-warbler is more often seen than heard, and for this reason is not easy to watch, for it lives in the undergrowth or among the thick vegetation which springs up so quickly in the later weeks of spring. But the male can often be seen sitting on a favourite perch, which is usually a twig on an osier just above the grasses or hedge parsley ; he will use this all through the nesting season, sitting there and singing while his mate is sitting, and also, before that, using it to proclaim his territory with many strange mixtures of bird notes. I have never seen sedge-warblers fighting before the females arrive ; they appear to live a very peaceful life, and mate up very soon after the hens put in an appearance, which may be two or three days after their arrival. The main body of these warblers arrive within two or three days of each other, a few stragglers dropping in during the first or second week of May.

It is my belief that the same birds attempt to use the same territories each spring. If both

Sedge-warblers at nest

Inset top.—Female Sedge-warbler which fell exhausted over her young

[88

male and female manage to survive the perils
of migration I believe they will mate up again.
An interesting incident was to be seen in a
small isolated bush on the side of one of the
Tring reservoirs. For three seasons in succession
a pair of sedge-warblers built their nest in this
bush and succeeded in rearing their young.
The bush was in a very sheltered position and
each nest survived, although when the third
was built number one was rather badly
dilapidated, but sufficiently intact to show that
it was a nest. All three nests were within a
circumference of three feet, so it was possible
to place the outspread hand in such a position
that all three could be touched. My belief
is that it was the same pair of warblers
which used this bush in three successive
seasons.

The nest is usually within a couple of feet
of the ground, but I have found it eight feet
above; it is rather bulky, but compact, and
quite different to the neat home of the reed-
warbler, which is usually suspended on two or
three reed stems, grasses or twigs. When built
in the matted undergrowth or thick vegetation
it usually has some support underneath it, but
once I found it suspended on two twigs like
that of the reed-warbler. The eggs—four, five
or six—are spotted all over with fine, ocherous
marks, with more round the larger end, while

near the top we nearly always find a few fine dark streaks, like markings which might be made with a fine mapping pen filled with black ink. It has been stated that two broods are sometimes reared, but I have never known this to occur, for after the end of June there are very few nests to be found containing young, and those which I have found have belonged to pairs which have accidentally lost their first nest. The period of incubation is thirteen days at the few nests that I have timed, but eggs hatched in an incubator have taken fifteen days. I doubt, however, if the latter would give a correct rendering of the time taken in nature. Most of the eggs of the warblers and other small birds found in our woods and fields take thirteen days.

The song of the sedge-warbler can only be confused with that of the reed-warbler, and I find very little difficulty in separating the two. The former is harsher, and if we wait patiently close to the singer he will sooner or later show himself, while the reed-warbler will sing for hours from the depth of a thick reed-bed without being seen. He is a fine mimic, and often on dark spring nights I have heard him holding forth, bringing in the songs or call notes of other birds. Owing to his habit of singing at night he has been mistaken for

the nightingale, but only by those who know very little about bird song. I was once told that a nightingale was singing near a stream in Wales, but investigation showed that it was the sedge - warbler. One good test of finding if the bird is actually a sedge-warbler is to wait until he stops singing, give him a few minutes' peace, then throw a small pebble into the bush or vegetation where he is ; if it is a sedge-warbler he will instantly take up the challenge and utter some excited notes. Without hearing the song, the bird can easily be distinguished by the broad stripe through the eye, the broad black stripes on its crown, and by the general reddish - yellow appearance, which seems to be almost a golden brown when seen with the sun shining on the plumage.

When the nest contains young, both parents feed them, taking it in turns to brood over them when quite small. At most of the nests that I have watched and photographed I have noticed that if the hen is brooding, directly she hears the other approaching, she slips off to make way, and he first gives the food he has brought to the young then takes his turn upon them, and so they carry on all through the day. Although I have waited with my camera at many nests I have seldom been able to obtain a picture of both birds feeding the young at the same time. I have seen the sedge-warbler arrive at the nest after a busy day, then appear to fall exhausted over her young in the same way that the whitethroat did on another occasion, and which I have already described.

I have not known the male sedge-warbler to build dummy nests during the period his mate is sitting, but this may be because of the difficulty of finding them in the thick undergrowth. His near relation, the reed-warbler, will build two and sometimes three dummies, all close to the nest actually used. The nest is easy to find, for it is usually within a few feet of the perch on which the male sings. I have found far more nests by watching the birds than by actually searching, for if we remain still in their haunt the male is sure to give away the site, either by taking food down to his sitting mate, or dropping down to the nest to take his turn upon the eggs. The female does all the building; he will stand by and sing, but does not appear to assist her in any way. The foundation consists of moss and dry grasses, while the nest itself is built of dry stalks and grass. The rough nest is first made, then the hen going inside works her body round and round, meanwhile placing the materials in position with her beak; eventually quite a neat little home is made, well fastened to its supports. During the

period the young are in the nest the male
sings very little, but when they leave and
are able to look after themselves he will
occasionally break out again with a few bursts
of snatchy song.

The Song - Thrush

Description.—Length, 9 inches. Upper parts, olive-brown; head, slightly redder; under parts, white, or buff-white, covered with distinct brown and black blotches; eyes, chestnut; legs, yellowish-brown.

Field characters.—Can be distinguished by general olive-brown appearance and distinct spots on breast. In spring and summer can only be confused with the mistle - thrush, but the latter is larger, has a greyer appearance, and breast spots are larger and not so rounded as those of the song-thrush. The song is distinct, and described in chapter.

IN parts of England this popular bird is known as the throstle and in Scotland as the mavis. I like the latter name, it is so much more musical than thrush, and seems to fit a bird with such a lovely song.

Many years ago I was staying in a small Scottish village in search of certain birds to be found in that district. Our headquarters were a delightful little inn, one of those places where the traveller was made so welcome in those far-off pre-war days, and where the fare offered was superior to that found in most of the modern village hotels. The day after our arrival the village belle was married to a local fisherman, and in the evening the whole male population of the village repaired to our inn and made

merry until late at night. After all these years
I have a dim recollection of the evening's
events, except that songs of all descriptions
were bawled out with such power as only
fishermen can put forth, to the accompaniment
of a rusty concertina, sometimes following the
singer, but more often not! But there is one
item that does stand out very vividly, and that
was an old song sung by a fisherman with a
delightful tenor voice. When he commenced a
silence fell upon the crowd and even the
accompanist ceased to play, and we listened to
those beautiful words :

> " I have heard the mavis singing
> His love-song to the morn,
> I have seen the dew-drop clinging
> To the rose just newly born."

The singer received a rough but well-
deserved encore and sang the same song again,
and whenever I hear the thrush called the
mavis, my thoughts go back to that little
Scottish inn, nestling among a few cottages on
a wild part of the northern coast.

The song-thrush is known from one end of
these islands to the other. I have listened to
its song in some of the wildest and most desolate
parts of Scotland and Wales, and also in the
heart of crowded towns, for there are few
places where we do not find this fine singer
if there are a few bushes or trees to attract

Song-thrush at nest

Inset.—Song-thrush in snow and nest " snowed out "

him. In the Outer Hebrides its place is taken by a darker variety called the Hebridean song-thrush. I have often heard this latter bird singing, and there is practically no difference in the song; if anything the notes are louder and more pure, but this is a characteristic of all thrushes which we find on the hills close to the sea.

I suppose I have been asked hundreds of times how to distinguish the song of the thrush from that of the blackbird. The two songs are absolutely different. The notes of the blackbird are lower in tone, it might be called a contralto song, and the actual notes are a rambling mixture. Those of the song-thrush are repeated several times, and it is easy to put his notes into words. As the singer sits on a topmost twig of a tree we hear each bar repeated three and sometimes four times, while if he happens to strike a special bar which is more attractive to him than the others he will repeat it five times. The notes are like the words "pretty-dick, pretty-dick, pretty-dick," and a variety of others which the imaginative observer can soon translate into our language. I was once photographing a dabchick from a hide on a large reservoir. As I was taking cinema films at the time, and wanted plenty of variety in my pictures, I had rather a lengthy wait; but the hours went by quite pleasantly, for

among other bird notes to entertain me a
thrush in a bush nearby sang all through the
day, and every few minutes he called loudly
" stick-to-it, stick-to-it, stick-to-it ! " And often
since then, while I have been waiting in my
hide in the woods or fields, I have listened
to those popular and certainly cheering
notes which seemed to be telling me not
to give in.

Those of my readers who have read that
delightful book by H. V. Morton, *In Search of
England*, will remember that charming little
incident where a thrush chided the writer
for parting with a tin of petrol. In a book which
interested me more than any written in modern
times this incident stands out strongly, for
it shows how easily the notes of the thrush can
be interpreted into words.

The varied song of this bird is some of the
finest avian music to be heard in the country,
some prefer it to that of the nightingale, and on
many occasions the thrush has been mistaken
for that singer. The nightingale usually sings
from a branch which is not more than twenty
feet from the ground, and he is often well
concealed among the leaves ; on the other
hand, the bold song-thrush likes to get right to
the top of the tree, and there on an exposed
branch he sits, seeming as though he was
trying to throw out his fine music to the whole

world. The best time to hear the song is on a
fine spring or early summer evening while his
mate is sitting on her eggs beneath. He will
sing from the same twig night after night, for
his territory is not a large one; a tract of
country fifty yards square will suffice, and all
through the period of incubation, and during the
feeding period when the young are in the nest,
all the food is collected inside this domain.
We have three pairs in our garden, that is three
to an acre of ground, and each pair keep to
their respective feeding grounds. The pair
which this year (1932) reared three broods in
the north end collected their food from the
vegetable garden and a small lawn; those at
the south end, which also had three broods,
found most of their food on the tennis lawn;
while the third pair, which had the centre of
the garden, discovered plenty of worms and
other food on the grassy banks. One morning,
when food was not too easy to find, one of the
thrushes belonging to the centre territory
poached upon the tennis lawn, and a fight took
place; the two combatants faced each other
for about a minute, then, as though at a given
signal, they flew together and rose straight up
into the air for a height of fifteen feet or so, and
after a tussle in the air went back to the lawn;
this was repeated several times until the poacher
went back to his or her own territory. Apart

from this little incident, the birds appeared to keep strictly to their own tracts. Over forty young thrushes were reared in the garden, but now at the end of the nesting season there are very few about. When the young thrush leaves its nest it advertises its presence to such an extent, by repeatedly uttering a loud, harsh and unmusical note, that any enemies on the look-out for young birds would have little difficulty in finding them.

The mortality among young birds is very great. Out of every dozen reared in the nest I doubt if four survive. There are so many enemies on the look-out for them, they are such easy prey, and we find weasels, stoats, cats, grey squirrels, rats and many of the larger birds searching for them most diligently, from the beginning of May to the middle of July. The majority of these enemies do not, however, have too easy a time, for whenever they approach a territory occupied by one of the smaller birds the note of alarm is instantly given out, and no matter what the species of bird is, this is a general note understood by all, and numbers flock to the spot and warn every youngster within hearing that danger is near. It is remarkable how the young know exactly what to do the instant they hear the warning signal. I have seen young birds not out of their shells for more than three or four hours squat down and remain motionless until they heard the signal which denoted the coast was clear. One English naturalist quotes a remarkable instance of this. He was watching a young moor-hen emerging from its shell. During the period of escaping the mother gave her cry of alarm, and the young bird, which had only partially escaped, at once ceased its struggles and kept still until danger was past.

The nest of the song-thrush is built chiefly by the hen, and most of the construction is done in the morning. The male will assist by bringing material to her. The foundations consist of grasses, roots and sometimes moss, strengthened with mud and clay. During the periods of building, and when the cup is formed, the birds collect beakfuls of wet mud or clay and place this at random around the inside ; while this material is still wet the hen goes inside and turns her body slowly round, pressing her breast against the interior. In this way she is able to work the mud smooth, then more grasses may be added and another layer of clay. The final lining consists of clay or mud, worked smooth in this way, while on the extreme outside she gives an extra smooth touch by mixing rotten wood or dry dung with saliva. The whole nest is a very neat structure, and the lining a hard one for eggs, but very few ever appear to become damaged.

All kinds of situations are used, hedgerows, clumps of ivy, isolated bushes, outhouses and garden sheds. In some parts of the country there is a type of thrush which builds on the ground. I know one wood near my home where each year we find several nests constructed right on the ground, usually at the base of a small tree. Season after season these same thrushes build on the ground, although there is an abundance of bushes for them if they desired to use them. In market gardens thrushes will often build on the ground under the large clumps of rhubarb. I have seen many in this situation, also on grassy banks.

The blue eggs of the song-thrush with their black spots make them some of the most beautiful of our British eggs. They vary in the brilliance of the blue and also in the number of spots; some have the latter nearly or quite absent, while a variety has been found with an almost white ground with reddish-brown markings.

The young remain in the nest about a fortnight, not less than this time if left undisturbed. Large numbers, however, leave the nest before they should; perhaps a weasel visiting the spot, or a rambling cat passing by, will induce the parents to attract their young from their home before they can fly properly. These youngsters will sit in prominent positions on fences, the outside branches of bushes, and soon fall a prey to their enemies. The young are very voracious and will devour large quantities of food ; the chief food given to them consists of worms, which the parents seem to have a wonderful gift for discovering at all hours of the day, even in dry weather.

When the young commence to fly and follow their parents about they are taken to the meadows and lawns, where they are shown how to find and capture worms. One young bird that I was watching caught a worm considerably longer than itself. However, this did not seem to deter it from trying to swallow it ; after a struggle, with many big gulps, the worm disappeared down the spacious throat, but the youngster forgot to close its beak, and the dire result was that the worm wriggled out ! The baby bird now looked at the wriggling creature on the ground, examined it carefully from every angle, and no doubt came to the conclusion that it was a second worm ! Not being overburdened with the first, which it thought it had swallowed, it made another attempt, and exactly the same thing happened ! But young birds are quick to learn their lessons, and on the worm going down for the third time and disappearing from view, the youngster kept its beak closed and the worm was not seen again !

I have often been amazed at the number of worms young thrushes can dispose of while they are in the nest. I have watched the parents bring big bunches in their beaks at ten-minute intervals and keep this up for three hours, but one or more of the family were always ready for food. These youngsters must eat several times their own weight of food during each day. Many adult birds will do this. The robin, for instance, will consume more than its own weight of food every day of its life if it is able to find it ; while the kingfisher can easily beat this, for I have known one to eat just about four times its own weight of fish in twenty-four hours.

At some nests that I have watched the hen has done most of the feeding, while at others the duties have been equally divided. My hide may have accounted for the shyness of the male at some of these nests. For accurate bird watching the observer must be thoroughly concealed, and the birds must not know of his presence.

Sometimes, when feeding their young, birds are faced with little problems, and it is interesting to see how they solve them. While waiting concealed at one nest the male thrush arrived with a large cockroach ; he was holding the creature across the middle of its body, and he tried to place it in one of the wide-open beaks. As the cockroach refused to bend, it lodged across the base of the beak and could not go down. He pushed and pushed, then tried another beak, it would not go down that —and so he went all round the nest. What was he to do ? He stood there looking quite disappointed that this fine beakful could not be disposed of, and once it looked as though he was going to solve the problem by swallowing it himself. All the time the five youngsters were clamouring for the food, and again he attempted to put it down an open beak, but each attempt was a failure. He suddenly thought of a new method : as the cockroach was wriggling all this time he could not leave go, so, placing his head on one side, he was able to force it head-first down a baby thrush's beak, and to prevent it wriggling back he pushed it well down ! I thought the youngster would choke, but not so, for with a few big gulps the cockroach completely disappeared, and, having succeeded in his task, the male thrush flew away for another supply of food. Fortunately I had my cinema camera fixed up in my hide, so I was able to obtain a record of this interesting scene in the home-life of one of our most popular birds, and thousands have been able to look upon it.

The cleverest problem that I ever saw worked out by a bird concerned a merlin.

This dashing little moorland falcon had one of its legs caught in a noose. For some time it struggled madly, then, finding that it could not escape in this way, it stood on the ground and looked at the knot round its legs ; it examined it from all points, moving its head from side to side as it did this, then it began to carefully pull at the string and, finding that the noose holding it became loose, it continued until the knot had been opened so much that it was able to step out and escape.

The parent thrushes are very bold in attacking enemies. I have had them fly at my head when I have been near their nest containing young ; they will actually strike cats and dogs, darting down at them from behind, and endeavouring to peck at their backs as they fly past. Their near relation, the mistle-thrush, is even bolder still, for I have known one to strike at a cat with such force that pussy thought the best plan would be to bolt from the spot. I have watched many fights between mistle-thrushes and jackdaws when the latter have been trying to rob the nest, and the thrushes are usually victorious.

The song of the mistle-thrush cannot be confused with that of the song-thrush ; the former is more like that of the blackbird, consisting of deep, rambling notes. It is, however, a fine song and a very welcome one, because it comes early in the spring, in fact we may often hear it on bright mornings in January. We have a pair in our garden, and the male will perch on the top of a tall cherry-tree and hold forth for minutes at a time, especially if a long burst of sunshine follows rain.

Song-thrushes vary very much in their song. I sometimes wonder if it is the younger birds which are so inferior; their notes are not so distinct and are repeated perhaps only twice, and are much harsher than the clear, ringing notes of a good singer. The finest singer I ever heard sang from the top of a tall poplar over the old village where I lived. The village itself was a delightful rural retreat, and some of my happiest days were spent there.

When the thrush first began his spring song the poplar had no leaves upon it; winter seemed to have hardly gone when the first sunny day of spring arrived, and the sudden warmth called many birds out to try over their summer notes. I do not know how many years past the thrush had sung from this same perch, but we were all glad to hear his first notes again. There was no mistaking this thrush when he began, for he had a wonderfully clear and loud song.

This charming old English village stood among beautiful surroundings, and as the thrush sang he looked down upon a maze of green meadows, three lakes and woodland. In the middle of the spring-time we saw delicious shades of green there, no two trees alike, and the tall reed-border fringing the lake had waves of colour sweeping over it as the wind played over the water. Beyond the lake were the red-roofed cottages, and the ancient church stood above them like a sentinel of the ages. The meadows between looked like carpets of gold as the buttercups faced the sun, while over all there was a great chorus of bird music— but above all we heard the notes of our bird. We called him the village thrush because he seemed to belong to it, and each spring as surely as we knew the leaves and blossom were coming so we expected him. There was no mistaking his song, there was not another thrush for a dozen miles round who could equal him for variety of notes or loudness and purity of song. I was listening to him early one April morning; the rising sun was shining into my room, and it was impossible to sleep with that bird not far from my open window. I counted twelve changes in his song, and many of the notes he repeated five times.

It is always interesting to listen to a fine singer like this. Sometimes he struck a new variety of notes, and immediately afterwards stopped as though he was trying to memorize them, but they were seldom repeated. Most of his bars were sung three times, but there was one glorious combination of notes that he often repeated five times. He began to sing from that high perch at the beginning of April, and for over three months he kept it up, giving out such music to that little English village that if it had been in a town thousands would have flocked to hear him. He was just part of the old village, and we listened to his song as we did to the clanging of the lock gates, the rush of water as the locks emptied to allow a barge to pass on, or to the deep tone of the church clock as it struck out the sixteen hours through which he sang to us.

There is no spot that I love quite as much as that old village nestling among those trees, meadows and lakes, and I love it best when the thrush sends out his loud notes over his small world to tell us that spring has come.

The Blackbird

Description.—Length, 10·5 inches. Upper parts of male, glossy black ; bill, bright orange-yellow, more brilliant in spring ; eyes, dark brown, with a thin orange line around ; legs and feet, dark brown ; upper parts of female, russet or umber-brown ; under parts, lighter brown, with dark markings or spots.

Field characters.—The bright orange bill and rim round the eye distinguish it from any other British bird; the male will often flick up his tail and duck his head while standing on the ground or other perch. The note of alarm is a loud " tchuk, tchuk, tchuk," repeated many times as the bird flies from the danger.

THE brilliant black plumage of the blackbird, together with his loud warning cry, given on the slightest sign of danger, are familiar to all dwellers in the country. Both the blackbird and its near cousin the song-thrush seem to like human company, and more nests will be found close to houses bordering woods and coppices than in the open country.

Why is it that many birds, which look upon man as their enemy, will often nest close to human habitations ? It may be because the other enemies, such as squirrels, stoats, etc., are shy of approaching such spots, but on the other hand there is usually a cat in evidence, which is one of the very greatest enemies of bird life.

In the early spring, even in February if the

111

weather happens to be mild, the male blackbirds commence fighting. These early fights are evidently to decide the territories, for the blackbird, after he has settled down in his domain, will guard it against all comers. The fights are not fatal, as sometimes happens with some of the smaller birds, there is a great amount of show, a lot of noise, but little damage is done. During some of these bouts the combatants will cease their fighting and continue to feed with their companions. During the winter months we see many more males than females, and in February and March they are also in the majority. Many of the birds reared in the country move southwards on the approach of winter, while those from farther north take their place. These males are probably visitors, for we see eight or ten on the lawn at once, but there is seldom more than two pairs to be found in the garden in the nesting season. For each six males we see one hen. Do the males remain behind while the females move southwards ? There are hundreds of problems of this description to be worked out regarding the habits of our commonest birds, and the excellent ringing scheme organized by Mr. H. F. Witherby, the Editor of *British Birds,* is doing a lot to solve them. The movements of our birds in every season are being carefully recorded and much valuable information is being collected.

Male Blackbird at nest
Inset.—Female

The Blackbird

The blackbird's territory is larger than that occupied by the thrush; he goes farther afield to find the food for the young, although the actual food collected is the same as that collected by the song-thrush. The latter comes out fearlessly into the open to collect its food, but the blackbird is far more shy; during the whole of the nesting season we seldom see the female blackbird, although there are two pairs in the garden each spring, and they each rear several broods. The thrush, after it has collected a beakful of worms from the lawn, will fly openly to its nest, but the blackbird slinks through the bushes and arrives at the nest without being seen.

All kinds of situations are occupied for nest building—hedges, bushes, ivy-covered walls, in trees and on the ground. I have seen a nest thirty feet up a chestnut-tree, and another in a cabbage. The latter was built on top of the heart, and the large leaves above completely hid the sitting bird. I have often seen the nest on the ground on grassy banks; this is a favourite spot in the early spring before the leaves appear on the hedges. Each spring I find several nests of blackbirds and thrushes built in very exposed situations in the hedges. I often wonder if these are the nests of those birds which are nest-building for the first time, and have had no experience of the numerous

H 113

inquirer told me that she had a white blackbird in her garden, and it had been with them for several seasons. She then asked me if I could tell her if one of its parents was a sea-gull !

The blackbird is one of the first to give the alarm if an enemy should show itself in his territory. His loud, rattling cackle, which it is not easy to put into words, might be described as " tchuk, tchuk, tchuk " repeated many times and usually during flight. It has the effect of putting all the other wild creatures within hearing on the alert, and if he continues, the other birds flock to the scene and join in the noise. If the male blackbird discovers a brown owl roosting in a tree in the wood, he will arouse the whole neighbourhood, and I have seen the birds gathered around, so noisy and persistent, that the large bird has flown off to endeavour to find peace elsewhere, but the noisy birds follow, and altogether the owl must have a very uncomfortable time.

The blackbird's song is most mellow and beautiful ; with some bird-lovers it comes first among our British birds. It is given from a high branch and several bars are uttered, then the singer flies on to another high perch, travelling all over his territory, seeming as though he wishes to give each part a portion of his song. The song itself is a rambling collection of notes, the singer is the contralto

116

in our bird chorus, and when heard on a calm spring evening, with a glorious sunset as a background to the stage, it is a song set in such a scene that it lingers long in our memory. The only song that we can confuse with it is that of the mistle-thrush, and sometimes the songs are so much alike that I have had to see the singer before I could decide.

mistle-thrushes will occupy a tract of land covering five or six acres, and they are exceedingly jealous of other birds, or in fact any wild creatures interfering with them. The courting of this large thrush takes place in January or early in February. The male makes plenty of noise, notes composed chiefly of his alarm cry, and these are evidently a challenge to other birds which may approach him. I have not seen any special display, except showing off in the common manner by slightly lowering his wings, raising his tail, and slowly approaching the bird he wishes to woo. These minor displays are constantly broken off, to allow him to again utter his loud cry of anger, as a song-thrush or blackbird passes by.

The nest is built in a fork of a tree, or on a large horizontal branch of a tall oak or elm. In Scotland I have found the nests a few feet from the ground in small fir-trees on the margins of plantations, while those birds which frequent rocky coasts will often build in clefts of rocks which are covered with vegetation. The eggs are usually four in number, sometimes five and rarely six. Their colour ranges from tawny-cream to greenish-blue, spotted and freckled with markings of brown and underlying markings of lilac; occasionally the eggs are very slightly or quite unspotted.

TH

Both male an
in defending th
of egg-stealing l
seen many a figh
jackdaws. In on
trying to obtain
was built on the
time after time t
nest, only to be
the end of the
giving up. The
the exceeding br

On a branch
west Ireland a
their home. The
the sea, the v
milder than fartl
for the birds l
February.

Down below,
the undergrowth
was fully twenty
was a magnifice
were cat-like in
sniffing to right
was carried well

The hunter w
it is so scarce t
last haunts are
largest forests.

Mistle-thrush

Inset.—Nest and eggs

[120

object, which was evidently giving it pain, then remained standing on his hand for a few seconds. But now, finding that the help wanted had been rendered, it flew off, settled in a tree about two hundred yards away, and several times repeated its loud contralto song.

Male Linnet at nest
Inset.—Female

The Linnet

Description.—Length, 5·5 inches. Male : upper parts, back
chestnut, lighter on rump and streaked with white; forehead and
middle of crown, crimson;   the rest of the head, greyish-brown;
wings and tail, much darker brown, the feathers having whitish
margins; under parts, breast, crimson; remainder, dull white,
the chin being striped with greyish-brown; bill, brown; eyes,
hazel; legs and feet, brown.   The female is generally duller than
the male, has no crimson on head and breast, and upper and under
parts are streaked with dark brown.   In both sexes the plumage
varies considerably, some of the males being much brighter with
more crimson than others.

Field characters.—Found frequently during spring and early
summer on furze-covered commons, and large tracts of open
country containing plenty of scrub and undergrowth, at other
times seen in considerable flocks.   When disturbed the birds
rise with undulating flight, all uttering a sweet twitter.   The
white wing bars and white margins of tail feathers often noticeable
during flight, especially so with the male birds ; in spring and summer
the bright crimson crown and breast distinguish the male.

THE linnet is one of the best of our lesser
songsters, its sweet and continued twitter seems
to be part of our gorse-covered commons.
In England it is common, being found in
most country districts where there is suitable
ground for nesting, and this may consist of
any little open tract of woodland with thick
undergrowth, corners of fields overgrown with
brambles, and especially commons, fields or
roadside banks covered with gorse bushes.

127

It can easily be induced to nest in a corner of a large garden, or in paddocks, by placing a few branches of fir-trees in the ground in the form of a small canopy. Half a dozen spreading branches stuck in the ground with their tops meeting will suffice, and not only linnets but thrushes, hedge-sparrows, blackbirds and, in marshy districts, sedge - warblers will take advantage of these covers. I knew one little coppice where about a dozen of these canopies were fixed, and although they were only a few yards apart, almost every one was used by a bird of some description for nesting purposes. In one three birds had actually taken up their abode, a wild duck on the ground and two pairs of smaller birds in the cover above, which, as far as I can remember, were linnets and blackbirds.

The courtship of the linnet is pretty to watch. The male approaches the hen with drooping wings and spread tail, repeatedly raising both and vibrating the tips of the feathers very rapidly. Sweet, low notes are uttered, and during this display the hen seems to take absolutely no notice of his advances. She sits on a twig near, preens her feathers and attends to her toilet generally, while all the time the male is doing his best to attract her attention. I really believe that, although she appears to be ignoring him, she is doing what maidens do the world over, she is watching him very carefully out of the corners of her eyes, for if he seems to tire of this display and flies off she is very careful to follow, and this induces the male to increase his efforts. Occasionally he will fly to an exposed twig, and sitting there and swaying backwards and forwards, he gives out his sweetest music, but he will not do this if he knows he is being watched by human eyes.

It is not easy to define the territory occupied by a pair of linnets. From observation it seems to me that a small party of these birds will occupy the same tract, all keeping inside that territory, while on another part of the nesting ground there will be another group of, say, half a dozen pairs, and these do not trespass on the feeding grounds of the former. These family parties live in agreement, the males do not appear to fight, and the nests are often only a few feet apart.

The nest is well concealed, usually not more than three feet from the ground, sometimes actually on it. It is built of stalks, moss, bents, fine roots and lined with hair and wool, with sometimes a few feathers. It is a cosy, well-built little home. The eggs are bluish-white, with spots and a few small streaks of purplish-red; blue and white varieties quite free from spots have sometimes been found. In number they vary from four to seven.

why it is valued as a cage-bird, for if other good singing birds are kept in close proximity it will soon pick up many beautiful notes which it incorporates in its own song. The song is often given from the seclusion of a bush, but if we are careful not to show ourselves, we can often see it perched on the topmost twig of a gorse or other bush, singing lustily, and a handsome bird he appears with the sun shining on his crimson breast.

When the young appear in the nest both birds look after them most carefully. While searching for food they are usually absent from the nest for forty minutes, but during the first five days one bird remains to brood over the young, covering them while the other is away in the fields collecting seeds and, occasionally, very small insects. On its return, if it happens to be the female bird, the male will rise from the young and stand on the side of the nest, fluttering his wings and uttering sweet, low notes while his mate is giving the food to her family. On arriving with food we do not see any in the bird's beak, but when she commences to feed a liquid which from my hides, usually a distance of ten feet, looks like milk, is very carefully given to each youngster in turn. Many birds when they reach the nest place all the food they have brought into the first wide-open beak they see. Thrushes, blackbirds

and the warblers will do this, so it is a welcome
change to see a small bird taking so much
trouble to feed each baby in turn. If the food
holds out she will go round to each youngster
three times, then when all this partly-digested
food is consumed she settles down on the nest,
and the male flies off for his supply. And so
they take it in turns all through the day. I
have waited for hours at many nests of the
linnet, and I never tire of watching this pretty
scene in their home-life. On one occasion the
male returned with a good supply of food and
settled on the side of the nest on which his
mate was brooding; directly he arrived she
stood up, opened her beak, fluttered her wings
and uttered low twitterings. He did not
hesitate a moment, but passed all the food over
to her; this operation took nearly a minute,
then she passed the food on to the young, while
he stood by and looked on. When all had been
given to them he rubbed his beak against hers,
uttered a few bright notes, and flew off to search
for another supply. This was a delightful
little scene, for while she was feeding the
family he showed his pleasure with many happy
flutterings of his wings.

There are few days in the year when we do
not hear the merry twitterings of linnets in our
garden, for it is a common bird in this district;
every bird which enters our garden is encouraged

and protected. It will give some idea of what this encouragement will do when I state that although the garden is only just over one acre in extent we have had thirty-five different species of birds nesting in it, or within a dozen yards of it, in the meadow just outside. Nesting boxes are placed on the trees, while in the bushes and other suitable spots old tins, kettles and boxes are fixed up, and practically all are used each year, while in the winter months a bird-table is there with a supply of food for all comers.

The farther north we go the scarcer the linnet becomes, although the only place it is rare appears to be on the west side of Scotland, but this year (1932) it has appeared and nested on tracts of moorland where it has not previously been seen.

Robert Burns was familiar with this delightful little songster, for he has immortalized its song in those beautiful lines :—

> " I wadna gie the lintie's sang
> Sae merry on the broomy lea,
> For a' the notes that ever rang
> From a' the harps of minstrelsie.
> Mair dear to me, where buss or breer
> Amang the pathless heather grows,
> The lintie's wild, sweet note to hear,
> As on the ev'nin' breeze it flows."

Male Chaffinch at nest

The Chaffinch

Description.—Length, 5·75 inches. Male : upper parts, head, bluish-grey ; back, chestnut ; rump, yellowish-green ; wings, dark brown with two conspicuous white bars ; under parts, rich reddish-brown ; bill, lead colour ; eyes, hazel ; legs and feet, brown. Female : upper parts, dull brown, greyish on breast ; wings have white bars, as in male.

Field characters.—In summer can easily be distinguished by its loud call note, " pink-pink " ; very confiding, coming up to our houses to feed on crumbs and other food. If disturbed by the nest utters a loud whistle " pui," repeated many times. In flight, which is undulating, the white bars on wings are quite distinct.

THE chaffinch is one of the commonest birds to be found in the country, being far more numerous than the house-sparrow. The latter is confined chiefly to towns, farm-houses and other houses in the country where there are suitable nesting sites, while the chaffinch is distributed all over these islands, there being few places where it is not found.

The song of the chaffinch is a short but popular one ; it has been very happily rendered into our language by the words : "In another month will come a wheatear." The loud cry, " pink-pink," is also a familiar sound in every country district. The birds vary in the quality of their song and in the number of times it is repeated ; a first-class singer is not considered perfect until he finishes the bar with the loud " pink - pink " ; this among bird fanciers is called the " Amen." Although I am always listening for this finish, I have seldom heard it.

The chaffinch's territory is confined to a tract of country about one hundred yards square, but the birds do not keep to it as strictly as some of the warblers and the nightingale, for when they are feeding their young they will fly a considerable distance in search of suitable food ; but each pair seem to have a certain well-defined route which they follow, one pair not trespassing on the feeding ground of the other.

The courtship of the male chaffinch is a violent one ; he is the sheikh of the bird-world. When he first makes advances towards a female he behaves in the usual bird-like manner, bowing before her, showing his fine wings and tail, and doing his best to attract attention ; but the lady chaffinch does not show that she is interested, and will often fly away. He follows and again tries to attract attention, but finding that most of his attempts are a failure he changes his tactics, and instead of a gentle wooer he becomes a veritable little sheikh. He flies at the hen, knocks her off

136

the branch on which she may be sitting, follows
as she flies away, and each time she settles he
attacks her in a most determined manner.
It does not take her long to understand that
this violent lover means to woo her, so she
responds to his efforts, sits on a twig and
gently flutters her wings. The effect on the
male is rapid, for he changes from a desperate
fighter to the most humble slave, and fawns
before her in the way he did at the commencement of this wooing; but if she shows the
slightest sign of slighting him he again
commences to use force. I have seen a male
bird in our garden treat the bird he was wooing
in a very rough way, but she seemed to take it
all as though it was part of the performance.
There is one great thing in the favour of this
sheikh-like lover. When the bird he wants does
show that she is willing to become his mate,
it would be difficult to find in the whole of
birdland a more devoted companion. He assists
her in building, in sitting on the eggs, and in
feeding the young, and if enemies approach the
nest, he becomes a bold bird and does his
best to drive them away.

The nest of the chaffinch is one of the most
beautiful to be found in this country; it is
small, compact and often very wonderfully
camouflaged, looking so much like its
surroundings that it is difficult to distinguish

137

Commencing with the middle of September, very large flocks come to this country from the Continent, spreading themselves over the various counties and joining up with our own flocks ; these visitors return to their own countries in March and early April.

A pair of Bullfinches at their nest

The Bullfinch

Description.—Male: length, 6 inches; upper parts: head, glossy black; back, bluish-grey; rump, white; wings, glossy black with a broad white bar; tail, glossy black; under parts: breast, bright brick-red; bill, black; eyes, dark brown; legs and feet, dark brown. Female: head, black; back, ash-brown; breast, reddish-brown, but not so brilliant as in the male.

Field characters.—More often heard than seen; when it comes into the open can easily be distinguished by the white rump, black wings and head. The call note is a single short plaintive piping.

THE male bullfinch in his spring plumage is one of the most brilliant of our British birds; if we see him in the sunshine his colours are startling, and remind one of some of the gorgeous birds of the tropics. It is generally distributed all over the British Isles where suitable nesting quarters are found. A favourite site is a tall hedge which has been left untrimmed for several years.

The bullfinch and its mate remain in their territory, which is not a large one, throughout the year. For ten years past we have had a pair in our garden, and they seldom wander far from it, sometimes travelling over an adjoining orchard of three acres. At all seasons of the year we see them on the garden paths

141

they succeed. A pair of hedge-sparrows in
our garden built four nests in one season before
they were successful in bringing up a family.
It is for this reason that we are able to find so
many nests in August. When I have suggested
to my friends that we should search for nests
at this time of the year they have been
surprised, but a careful search will seldom be
in vain. A few years ago I proposed to some
bird-loving friends that we should attempt
this task, but they were very sceptical; but
before we had searched a hundred yards of a
likely-looking hedge we had found three nests,
with the owners sitting on their eggs. Those
birds which fail to rear a family of young
earlier in the season find the task is much
safer when there is a thick screen of leaves to
hide their little homes. The egg-stealing birds,
such as magpies, jays and jackdaws, have by
that time given up their quest, for their young
are out of the nests, and there is plenty of
other food to be found in the fields.

After the bullfinches had lost their second
nest they did not seem to worry much, but
commenced their third. This also contained
four eggs, and they eventually hatched. I
found that both cock and hen sat on the eggs;
the male was often to be seen covering them
during the morning, he no doubt taking his
turn after the hen had been on all night, and

so giving her an opportunity to obtain a good meal. The parents fed their young at intervals of about twenty minutes all through the day, the male working just as hard as his mate. Occasionally the male would brood over the young, even when they seemed large enough to do away with this extra warmth.

One morning, when the young were about ten days old, I heard both bullfinches calling frantically. Most of the other birds nesting in the garden were also joining in the cries of distress, and I knew that an enemy was near. As quickly as I could I ran to the nest, climbed up the steep bank leading to the tall hedge, and was just in time to see a stoat slinking away. I was, however, too late to save the young; three had disappeared, while the third young bullfinch was almost dead by the side of the nest.

After this tragedy the hen seemed very depressed; for a week we saw her sitting on branches in the garden with her feathers bunched up, her head drawn into her breast, and her eyes partly closed. I was not really sorry that this mishap had occurred at their nest, for it gave me an opportunity of seeing what a devoted mate the male bullfinch can be. I have often been accused by my critics of giving my birds human traits, but those who have watched wild nature as I have done

Wren

The Wren

Description.—Length, 3·5 inches. Upper parts, rufous-brown, barred with darker brown ; wings and tail, darker than back ; over eye there is a dull white streak ; under parts, chin and throat, buff-white, the rest greyish-brown ; bill, dark brown ; legs and feet, light brown.

Field characters.—Easy to distinguish from any other British bird by its small size and dark brown appearance. The song is loud, usually given from some prominent low perch, and while singing the tail is upturned. The flight is straight, sustained for short distances only, and wing-flaps very rapid.

THE wren has been called the little bird with the big song, and it certainly has a remarkably powerful voice for such a diminutive bird. When singing it looks as if the singer thought himself the most important creature in the whole of the countryside, for his beak is raised, the small pointed tail is upturned over his back and, by the notes that pour out of his tiny beak, he appears to be trying to drown all the other bird music around.

This bird is distributed all over the British Islands except in the Outer Hebrides and St. Kilda, where the St. Kilda wren takes its place. When I first visited the Outer Hebrides over twenty years ago I was struck by the remarkable song of the wrens that I saw there. I have

149

whatever the origin of this remarkable custom,
it does not alter the fact that up to the time
when I was a boy it was a common custom in
all country districts, and on the morning of
St. Stephen's Day numbers of boys and men
armed with sticks, stones and any other weapons
they could get hold of hunted the hedgerows
and bushes for this harmless bird. If they
were successful in their quest the unfortunate
victim was fastened on a pole and carried
through the village streets, while they chanted
the following :

"The wren, the wren, the king of all birds,
St. Stephen's Day was caught in the furze ;
We hunted him up and we hunted him down,
We hunted him all about the town."

Fortunately better education and the
introduction of nature study in some of the
schools has done away with this wanton
cruelty in most districts, although I believe it
is still carried on in a few places in the West of
England.

The nest of the wren is a cunningly-built
one, domed over at the top with a small hole
in the front just large enough to admit the bird.
It varies greatly in size, according to the
materials with which it is built. In some
woods I have seen it constructed almost entirely
of moss, in others dead leaves are used for the
foundations, while the smallest and neatest are

made of dead grasses and are built so cleverly that it is difficult to detect them from their surroundings. When built of dead bracken, as is often the case, the nest is much larger. All kinds of situations are used, such as the base of hedges, small bushes in woods, brambles, sides of stacks, under the roots of trees where the soil has fallen away, and in the old nests of other birds. The strangest situation I ever saw one in was inside the skull of a horse, which was lying on the ground in a corner of a vicarage garden.

My experience has been that if young birds have been reared in a strange place they will sometimes endeavour to find a similar place for their own nests when they build. Several instances of this have come under my notice, perhaps the most conclusive being connected with a pair of blue tits which nested in a lamp-post in a London suburb. The nest was built inside the iron pillar, and the young left their strange home successfully. Five years later at least half a dozen lamp-posts in that district were used by blue tits, and now, twenty-five years after the first pair nested, they are still carrying on.

The wren is not content with one nest, several are built each season, these extra homes being made by the male bird, and as a rule they are not lined with feathers as is the nest gardens, while in the heart of the country we will often find two pairs on an acre of ground. In my garden we have two pairs which keep strictly to their respective ends. One pair nest on the north side, and these usually select an old tin or kettle for the site of their home, while the other pair, living on the south side, nest on one of the grassy banks. Each pair rear at least two broods each season, but the numerous young brought up are not seen after the late summer. The young of all birds reared in these selected and well-guarded territories are probably driven farther afield by their parents, or it may be that they go off on their own account. Just outside the south end of the garden there is a third pair which nest on a bank, and on the north side a pair which usually select the roadside ditch for the site of their home. Apart from these four pairs there does not appear to be any increase in the numbers nesting on that tract of country.

The nest is rather a bulky structure, not unlike that of the nightingale, but with fewer dead leaves. The foundation will consist of dead leaves, but sometimes entirely moss, and the interior is lined neatly with hair and a few feathers. The eggs are white or pinky-white, covered with fine spots or freckles of sandy-red. In number they vary from four to seven, but even twelve has been recorded. This large

Robin in snow

number was evidently the work of two hens, for it will occasionally happen that two birds will lay in the same nest. This often happens with the partridge and some of our ducks. I once found a nest of a wild duck, and on visiting this a few days later I saw there was a second bird sitting by the side of the original owner. When the nest is built early in the season, as this was, and before there is little cover to hide the sitting bird, she usually sits very closely upon her eggs. These two birds actually allowed me to push them from their double nest, and I found that one bird had eleven eggs under her and the other nine. On visiting the nest a few days later I thought I would like to see if they had laid more eggs. I moved number one aside and found that she had fifteen eggs under her ; I thought she had done very well until I moved number two to discover that she had to be content with five only. These two ducks constantly shifted the eggs ; one day we found the first with a large clutch and the other with one or two and vice versa, but how many ducklings they brought between them I was not able to find out. Not very far from the site of this double nest there was a nest of the tufted duck containing twenty-eight eggs. How many ducks were responsible for this large number I never knew.

The robin is a very pugnacious bird and very

this enemy was after and eventually succeeding in getting.

In its habits the robin is very much like the nightingale. The two birds are closely related, but in the woods, where we find both, it is easy to distinguish them by their movements, even if we cannot see the distinguishing marks; the robin is very rapid in its movements, while the nightingale is far more deliberate. If we watch a robin on any perch, we will see that usually, just before flying away, it drops its wings and flicks its tail upwards, but the action is very rapid and not always easy to follow with the eye. The nightingale has exactly the same action just before flying from a perch, but we can describe it best by saying that it is performed in slow motion.

The song of the robin is so well known that it seems hardly necessary to describe it; there are very few weeks in the year when we do not hear it. The actual notes are musical, but somewhat plaintive, and consist of a warble lasting about five or six seconds.

There is no more homely bird than the robin; it has always sought out human company and likes to have its nest close to our houses. It becomes very tame, and will come into our rooms and feed from our hand. One that we had in our garden always came to me when I was gardening, for it knew that at such times

160

there would be plenty of hidden insects turned up. It would sit close to me and, with head cocked on one side, kept a sharp look-out for small worms or other creatures which hide in the soil.

In the winter months the male robins are just as jealous of their territories as in the spring; during one severe winter I saw the male from another territory approaching the one which frequented our then small garden. The latter was sitting on a branch on which I had placed some food. The visitor, being exceedingly hungry, decided to get some of this and flew to it, but the first bird placed itself in fighting attitude and dared the intruder to come nearer. For nearly a minute the birds sat there facing each other with lowered wings and beaks, with the food an equal distance between each, while both uttered the plaintive note of anger—" pheeze, pheeze." Eventually they flew at each other like little furies, to disappear into the hedge, still fighting. Ten minutes later my robin returned, so he had evidently succeeded in driving the trespasser away.

moment it had settled on a rock in mid-stream, and commenced bobbing its plump little body up and down in a remarkable manner. I knew at once that I was looking upon a dipper, and ever since that memorable morning this bird has always been a favourite of mine.

Since then I have seen, watched, and photographed many dippers in various parts of England, Scotland and Wales. The territory of a pair of dippers extends on many streams for about a mile. Observation shows that all through the year they keep to their stretch of water, seldom flying far from it over the moor. If a dipper wishes to fly from one part of the winding stream to another, it will usually follow the course of the water, and not take a short cut across country.

On some of the rivers in Wales the dipper has in late years become scarcer; what the cause of this is I cannot say, for, as far as I knew, the nests were not molested; on one or two rivers the birds have quite disappeared.

On one delightful estate in Scotland, where I have spent many happy weeks of my life, I have had good opportunities of watching the dipper. It was on one of the rivers there that I obtained my photograph which is shown here. I had fixed up my bird-watching tent close to a small rock on which it usually settled, but before going inside I thought I would place

164

Dippers

my finger in the nest to see how many young
there were ; to reach it I had to fix a petrol
tin in the water on which to put one of my
feet. On reaching to the nest I placed too
much weight on the tin ; this twisted round and
I had a ducking in ice-cold water ! However,
I was able to run back to the lodge, change my
clothes, and a short time after I was in my
tent watching the dippers returning to their
nest with food.

In collecting this the birds went right
under the swirling water, remained under for
just under one minute, then carried the food
they had found to the young ; the latter were
always ready for this, and before their parents
reached them there were several little heads
poking out of the nest entrance.

At other times I have watched the dipper
searching for its food. In one clear Welsh
stream I saw the bird go to the bottom ; then
it faced up-stream, allowing the water, which
was about a foot deep, to run over its body
from beak to tail ; now it walked slowly against
the running water, turned the small stones over
with its beak and snapped up small objects
which were washed out from under them. It
remained under each time for forty-five seconds,
but in that short time it was able to examine a
fair number of spots at the bottom of the river.

The nest of the dipper is a large structure ;

The Skylark and Woodlark

THE SKYLARK

Description.—Length, 7 inches. Upper parts, dark brown; small crest on head; tail, brown, the outer pair of feathers being nearly all white; under parts, buff-white, throat and sides of the neck are speckled; bill: upper, brown: lower, flesh - colour; eyes, dark brown; legs and feet, yellowish-brown.

Field characters.—Can be distinguished from the pipits by its larger size and slower method of travelling when on the ground. The longer tail and faint stripe through eye distinguish it from the woodlark. Song distinct and long continued.

THE WOODLARK

Description.—Length, 5·5 inches. Upper parts, brown; crest on head more distinct than on skylark; stripe over eye, distinct; tail short; two outer feathers, pale brown; next two pairs have white tips; under parts, creamy-white; throat and breast striped with dark brown; bill: upper, brown; lower, pale flesh-colour; eyes, dark brown; legs and feet, pale flesh-colour.

Field characters.—Short tail and the buffish-white eye-stripe meeting at nape and the pale flesh-coloured legs distinguish it from skylark.

OF all our British songsters the skylark and woodlark are the only ones that will sing continuously for long periods. The skylark rises from the ground with a glorious burst of lively song and goes up and up until out of sight, and long after we have lost sight of the singer we hear his notes. The lark has been known to remain in the air for half an hour,

169

one in full song on a stump of a broken-down fence. This was taken on the edge of a cliff on the Scottish coast. The woodlark, however, will often sing from a perch such as the top of a tree, telegraph wires, or a fence. I have heard one singing beautifully on a bright January morning ; all around me the ground was covered with snow, and although I was among the Welsh mountains at a height of over nine hundred feet above sea level, the bird was singing as though it was the middle of spring.

Both larks have their own well-defined territories. In districts where the skylark is numerous, such as some of the large meadows around my home, this tract of country will cover about three acres, but unlike the territories of other birds, it also extends to the sky. The skylark and woodlark look upon the space above their ground as their own property and resent other larks entering it.

The courtship of both birds takes place largely on the wing. In March if the weather is mild, and always in April, we see a male skylark following a female, uttering its twittering call note. The birds will twist and turn in the air, travelling at random over the meadows, but always returning to the territory selected by the male. On alighting, the male erects his crest, slightly lowers his wings and runs quickly around the hen, and if she shows signs of replying

172

Sky-lark singing on a post

Inset.—Sky-lark on ground

to this display he shows his pleasure by rising up towards the sky and giving out a burst of wild and joyous song. This display goes on for three or four days, sometimes even a week, before the birds settle down.

In their nesting habits the two birds are similar, but the woodlark will often have its first brood of youngsters in the nest before the skylark has laid her eggs. We find the nest of the former at the end of March, while the skylark usually has its eggs at the end of April. Both birds rear more than one brood, the woodlark will have two, and the skylark often brings up three separate families in the season. The nests of both birds are similar, being in small depressions on the ground, well concealed among growing grass or other vegetation. The woodlark prefers hill-sides, or the sides of woods where bracken abounds, also open, sandy country; while the skylark is a more homely bird, building in meadows close to houses, in growing crops on farms, and farm land generally. The materials used by both birds consist of bents and grasses, lined with finer grass and hair. The eggs of the skylark are a dull greyish-white, thickly speckled and spotted with olive-brown; those of the woodlark also have a greyish-white ground, but are covered with reddish-brown and olive-brown spots, with underlying markings of blue-grey; they are

173

After a heavy fall of snow we see large numbers of skylarks flying south. These pass over our garden for days in succession in parties of half a dozen or so, all flying into the sun, hoping to find a tract of open country which the snow has not covered.

Yellow-hammer

The Buntings

THE YELLOW-BUNTING

Description.—Length, 6·5 inches. Upper parts: head, on top and sides, yellow, streaked with brown; back, reddish-brown, wings, dark brown; tail, dark brown; under parts: yellow, the breast and flanks streaked with reddish-brown; bill, slate-blue; eyes, dark brown; legs and feet, light brown.

THE CORN-BUNTING.

Description.—Length, 7 inches. Upper parts, greyish-brown, feathers, darker in centre; streak over eye buff-white; wings, dark brown; tail, dark brown; under parts, buff-white; throat and breast, streaked with dark brown; bill: upper, dark brown; lower, yellowish-brown; eyes, dark brown; legs and feet, flesh-brown.

THE CIRL-BUNTING.

Description.—Length, 6 inches. Upper parts: head, on crown olive, black stripe through eye, forming a broad yellow streak above and below it; back, dark chestnut; rump, paler; wings, dark brown; tail, dark brown; under parts: chin and throat, black, under this a collar of sulphur-yellow, followed by broad olive-grey band; bill: upper, dark-brown; under, slate-blue; eyes, brown; legs and feet, yellow.

THE REED-BUNTING.

Description.—Length, 6 inches. Upper parts: head, black, with a deep white collar coming round to a point at the base of the bill; back, dark brown, the feathers having lighter borders; wings and tail, very dark brown; two outer pairs of tail feathers have white external margins; under parts, dull white, streaked with brown on the flanks; chin and upper breast, black; bill, dull brown; eyes, brown; legs and feet, brown.

Field characters.—The habits of all the buntings are somewhat similar. The yellow-bunting can best be distinguished by its song, which is described in chapter. The male has a general bright yellow

M   177

to its original perch to again sing. Most of the food that the birds require for themselves or their young can be found close to the nest and their territory is, therefore, a small one. An acre of ground would be a large tract for a pair, most are content with far less. The food consists of seeds of all kinds, but insects are also eaten and the young are fed upon caterpillars.

The nest of this bird is built on the ground, or a few inches above it, in scrub or furze; it is usually in an open field. The eggs are rather beautiful; the ground colour is greyish-white or very light brown, with bold brownish-black straggling lines.

The cirl-bunting greatly resembles the yellow-hammer in its habits and general appearance. The male can, however, easily be distinguished by the black throat and ear-coverts and the olive-grey band on its breast, but it is not too easy to distinguish the hen. A good field-glass will show her brown rump; that of the yellow-hammer is chestnut. The song is like that of the yellow-hammer with the long-drawn " che-e-e-se " omitted, or it can be compared with the loud ringing call of the lesser whitethroat. The eggs are not easy to distinguish from those of the yellow-hammer; if anything the markings are bolder.

The reed-bunting is one of our most

Reed Bunting.—Female on Branch

Inset.—Male

persistent singers, but there are few more unmusical or monotonous songs to be heard in the country-side. The bird is found in most marshy districts all over the country. The male is easy to distinguish with his black head and white collar, while his mate, usually seen not far from him, has a reddish-brown head. We see the male perched on a swaying reed, and uttering his song at half-minute intervals on the sides of lakes where these plants abound. At a distance both birds may be distinguished by their ragged appearance. The female, especially, will settle on a twig or reed-stem, spread and raise her tail, while her body appears to be at a ridiculous angle to it. With a jerk the bird will reverse its position and again spread the tail feathers.

The nest is placed in a clump of broken-down reeds or sedge, or in a bunch of matted vegetation, and is not too tidy a structure ; it is made of bents and moss, lined with finer grasses and a little horse-hair. I have seen many constructed chiefly, and lined, with the flower of the reed. The eggs number four to seven, but very rarely the latter number. Their ground colour is usually brownish-olive with a few bold streaks diffused all over the shell.

Incubation is undertaken by both birds, and when the young need brooding over the male takes his share. While photographing one pair I found that the male did most of the actual food collecting, but on arriving at the nest he passed it on to the hen and she gave it to the young. At the time the weather was very hot, the nest was also in an exposed situation, and I had to move some of the reed-stems aside to obtain my pictures. The mother evidently realized that if the hot sun shone upon her young for any length of time it would injure them, so she protected them in quite a clever manner. She gripped the top of one side of the nest with her left foot while her right was fixed on the other side, and for twenty minutes at a time she stood there with her wings partly open, so that the whole of the nest under her was in shadow. By standing in this manner instead of brooding directly on to the young she was able to make it far more comfortable for them, for the air circulated under her body. I have seen the reed-warbler behave in exactly the same way when a hot sun was shining on to her nest.

When the male arrived with food at this nest he first perched just under the flower at the top of a tall reed-stem, then with food in his beak he slowly descended by twisting downwards in a spiral, and sang loudly all the time. When he reached the undergrowth he slipped through, gave the food he had collected to his mate, and she left her uncomfortable position, handed the food to the young, and went back to her clever way of protecting them.

On the margins of the Tring reservoirs, where I have watched and photographed many pairs of these birds, I find their territories are very small. A patch of reed - bed, fifty or eighty yards square, will be quite sufficient for a pair, and in this they will remain all through the nesting season, rearing two and sometimes three broods.

The courting of the reed-bunting is done in the shelter of the bushes or among the tall reeds and it is not easy to follow, but I have seen the male making a slight display before the hen. He flutters towards her, vibrates the tips of his wing feathers and raises the black feathers on his head in the form of a crest ; he seems to shuffle along the branch as he approaches her, and from what I have been able to see, she takes very little notice of these advances.

Our resident reed-buntings move southwards in winter if the weather is severe, while their place is taken by visitors from the Continent. Those which leave return in March or early April.

The Titmice

THE GREAT TITMOUSE.

Description.—Length, 5·8 inches. Upper parts: head, glossy blue-black with small white spot on the nape; cheeks, white; back, yellowish-green; tail, bluish-grey; under parts: throat and sides of the neck, black; breast, greenish-yellow, with a broad black band running down from the throat; bill, black; eyes, dark brown; legs and feet, lead-colour.

THE BLUE TITMOUSE.

Description.—Length, 4·5 inches. Upper parts: top of head, cobalt-blue, encircled with a white band from the forehead; through the eye there is a dark-blue band which joins a collar of the same colour; cheeks, white; back and rump, yellowish-green; wings, blue; tail, blue; under parts, chin and throat, dark blue; breast, pale yellow; bill, almost black; eyes, dark brown; legs and feet, lead colour.

THE COAL TITMOUSE.

Description.—Length, 4·25 inches. Upper parts; head, on top and sides glossy black, with a bold white spot on nape; back, olive brown; wings, brown; tail, brown; under parts: throat and upper breast, glossy black; the rest, dull white; bill, black; eyes, brown; legs and feet, lead colour.

THE MARSH TIT.

Description.—Length, 4·5 inches. Head: on top and sides, glossy black; back, olive brown; wings, dark brown; tail, dark brown; under parts: chin and throat, black; breast, white; bill, black; eyes, brown; legs and feet, lead colour.

THE WILLOW TIT.

Description.—Like marsh tit, but can be distinguished by the head, which is a dull black instead of glossy.

THE LONG-TAILED TIT.

Description.—Length, 5¼ to 6 inches. Upper parts: head, white, with a black line passing from the bill over the eye to the back; back, black; rump, dull rose-red; wings, dark brown; tail, black; under parts: cheeks and throat, dull white; flanks and lower parts, dull rose-red; bill, black; eyes, brown; eyelids, orange-red; legs and feet, black.

Field characters.—The tits are easy to distinguish from other birds of their size by their acrobatic actions, sprightly movements and general smartness. The great tit is the largest of the species, and can be distinguished from other species by the broad black band extending down the front of breast. In the spring the great tit announces his presence by a continued loud musical call, " teach-er, teach-er, teach-er," and often by a clever imitation of the chaffinch's " pink-pink."

The blue tit is unmistakeable owing to its delightful cobalt-blue head and general blue appearance.

The coal tit is easy to distinguish from the marsh tit, which it much resembles, by the bold white mark on the back of its black head. In the marsh tit this is absent, the head being a complete glossy black, while the willow tit has a dull black head.

The long-tailed tit cannot be confused with any other British bird; its diminutive size and long tail are distinctive.

THE tits are more in evidence during the winter months. All are denizens of the woods and large orchards, and owing to their small size and often secretive habits they are not always easy to pick out when the trees are clothed in leaves, but during the spring months we hear their songs. These cannot be compared with the music given by the warblers and many other small birds, but they do add to the general chorus to be heard in our woods and gardens.

The loudest song is that given by the great

tit; the chief notes consist of two uttered in succession and can be described as " teach-er, teach-er, teach-er "; these two notes are a loud, musical-ringing call, and can be heard at a distance of two hundred yards. In the month of April when the males are declaring their territory we hear one bird answering another throughout the day. Besides these notes the bird gives another similar to the " pink-pink " of the chaffinch. Then there is a note which is shared by most of the titmice, described as " tsee, tsee, tsee." In the winter months, when the tits are in flocks, with tree-creepers and gold-crests, it is not easy to say which species is uttering the note.

If the weather is mild the great tit will begin his clarion call at the end of March, and if a hen shows herself in his domain he at once commences courting. The display consists of wing vibrations, with the tail lowered or raised, and he will often hold an insect in his beak as a gift for her. He becomes very noisy in the immediate vicinity of the nesting site, and if this is a nesting box will often settle outside it, as though he was inducing her to commence building.

These birds can readily be attracted to the garden by placing suitable nesting boxes for them; my illustration shows the kind we use. The box is about nine or ten inches deep and about six inches square; the top slopes downwards and comes well over the entrance hole to protect it from the wet; the top is hinged at the back, so that we are able to look at the inside when the birds are sitting, for they become very tame and allow us to stroke them as they cover their eggs.

We have two pairs in the garden each year, and they keep to their respective ends. The pair on the north side find practically all their food in the garden itself, while those on the boundary and south side go to an adjoining orchard for their supplies. They do not appear to often trespass in each other's territory. At the commencement of one nesting season a pair began their nest in box number one; when this was almost completed they left it to go to box number two, owing to another pair of great tits which drove them from this small territory. In this a nest was nearly finished, when again the aggressive pair decided that they were too near their own nest, which was in box number four. A third nest was built in box number three, this being the farthest box from number four, and here they were allowed to stay. The hen laid nine eggs in this, but during the period of laying she evidently could not forget her first choice, for she returned to box number one, which was now occupied by a pair of blue tits, and laid one egg in that.

Great Tit

Inset.—Male at nesting box

The blue tit also laid nine eggs and brought up nine youngsters of her own and one great tit. The other pair of great tits in box number four reared ten young.

The nest building is done chiefly in the early part of the morning; after ten o'clock very few visits with material are made. The male works quite as hard as the hen in collecting moss, hair, rabbits' fur and down; he takes the materials into the nesting box, but the hen does the actual constructing. Incubation lasts fourteen days, and is, I believe, done by the hen alone. During this period the male looks after his mate, bringing supplies of food to her.

When the young arrive both birds work hard in collecting food, which consists chiefly of caterpillars. Our garden is a wild one; a good part of it consists of an old pit from which sand has been extracted in the past; the banks are planted with fruit trees, while in other parts there is plenty of bramble and thick undergrowth. In this partly - cultivated wilderness the birds are able to find plenty of their favourite food. When the young are quite small either the male or female brood over them while the other is collecting food outside. After the first week the visits of both birds to the nest are constant; one day they came three times a minute and kept this up for

189

in March or early April, before the leaves appear which always hide so many incidents that we would like to follow. The male tries to attract the hen by uttering his merry song, then goes towards her with vibrating wings and raised crest; in this attitude he moves slowly round her, hopping from twig to twig, and she responds with similar wing vibrations.

The nest is commenced at the end of April, and all kinds of strange sites are selected. I have already mentioned in another chapter how a pair built in a lamp-post, and the descendants carried on in the same strange site. An old disused pump is a favourite place. I know one which has been occupied for many seasons. Holes in trees and stone walls are constantly used; tins left by the side of a hedgerow, letter boxes, or inverted flower pots are also favourite sites. Last spring (1932) we had a pair nesting in our garden in an old tin bottle; the entrance was just large enough for the birds to get through, and in this they reared a family of ten.

The nest is a cosy structure composed of moss with a little grass and lined with hair, wool and feathers. After each egg is laid the hen carefully covers them with the nest lining. The eggs vary in number from seven to twelve, but twenty-four have been found in one nest, evidently the produce of two hens. The eggs

Blue Tit

are very small, white, and usually covered with small, light chestnut spots, after forming a zone round the large end.

The young remain in the nest for at least three weeks if undisturbed by outside influences. In one nest in our garden the young could fly with ease at the end of a fortnight, but they all remained in their home for another eight days. The territory of a pair of blue tits is about one acre. After the young leave the nest they remain within the bounds of this for about a week, then they are led right away from the old site, the parents not seeming to appear again before the early autumn.

If a blue tit finds a dead bird during the winter, when food is not easy to discover, it will bore a hole in its head with its small, sharp beak, afterwards devouring the brains. The blue tit has been accused of killing other birds, but I doubt if it ever does or could do this; but it will ravenously attack the skull of a dead one. When I was a boy I witnessed a remarkable instance of this. Two blue tits were searching for food in a fruit tree; before I could prevent it one settled on a trap which someone had fixed in the tree and was caught and almost instantly killed. Even before it ceased to struggle the second bird pounced on to it, and commenced to peck at the skull to get at the brains !

The blue tit and other species of tits have been accused of doing harm in our gardens by breaking open the fruit buds in the early spring. Two years ago I watched a pair in our garden working up and down the branches of an apple tree. I saw them break open many buds, but I allowed them to continue, and later on in the year I had a fine crop of splendid apples on that same tree, which seemed to show that the birds were destroying only those buds which contained insect pests.

The song of the blue tit is a lively little strain, and it is heard from January to June. It can, I think, be described by the words " tsee-tsee-tsee-zit-it-it-it-it-it."

In recent years there has been a deal of controversy as to whether the marsh tit and willow tit should be separated as distinct species. The two birds are now recognized by ornithologists as distinct, for although they are alike in plumage, apart from one having a glossy black head and the other a dull black one, their songs are distinct and they differ in their habits.

The marsh tit will construct its nest in woods far from water, but my experience shows that the willow tit is never far from a river, lake or marsh. The marsh tit will generally build its nest in a hole of a tree which is already there, although I believe there have been

194

Willow Tit
Inset.—Marsh Tit

instances observed by others in which it bored a hole for itself in rotting wood. The willow tit will, as far as my personal observation goes, always make its own nesting hole, and this is not more than five feet from the ground, while the marsh tit will choose sites at greater heights. The materials used by both species for building are not quite the same. The marsh tit makes a foundation of moss, filling up the entire bottom with this, making a lining of rabbits' fur, down, and, if it can be obtained, small bunches of hair. The willow tit will use very little, if any, moss, with a smaller lining of down which is mixed with the wood-chips. A favourite site is a rotten willow stump close to water, by the side of an opening or ride, or a similar stump in a marshy wood. Stumps with a circumference of about twelve inches seem to be preferred to more solid ones.

The songs of the two birds are very distinct. I have known observers who are familiar with the songs of most of our popular birds to mistake the willow tit for the nightingale. It has one delightful note which is not unlike the " jug-jug " of the nightingale. The song commences with a series of harsh notes something like " chiz-chiz-chiz," followed by a very rich, mellow note which can be compared to the whistle which prefixes the wood-wren's song, but far more beautiful. This is repeated many times and is a really delightful addition to the general chorus of bird-song heard in the spring.

The song of the marsh tit is not so good; to my mind it more resembles that of the blue tit. I can best describe it as "zee-ip, zee-ip, zee-ip, chiz-iz-iz-iz-iz," with more of a musical tone.

Apart from the song, the willow tit can be distinguished from the marsh tit by its head. The feathers on both heads are black, but those of the willow tit are dull black, while those on the marsh tit are glossy. The coal tit can easily be distinguished from both, because at the back of its black cap there is a distinct white patch.

The following incident connected with a marsh tit may show that if a bird is taken from its territory it has difficulty in finding it again, although one experiment cannot be conclusive. A friend of mine found a nest of a marsh tit in the hole of a tree by the side of a Welsh river; this contained eggs and the bird was sitting upon them. He captured the tit, then carried it a mile from the nest and liberated it, the result was that it did not return to its eggs. I think a marsh tit would not desert its home simply because it was taken from the nest, for these birds are most persistent sitters and will return again and again if driven off. I believe that these small birds, which frequent such small territories, have no knowledge of the district as far as a mile from their home.

The Pipits

THE TREE-PIPIT.

Description.—Length, 6 inches. Upper parts, dark brown; under parts, chin, buff-white; breast, buff, spotted with dark brown; bill, dark brown; eyes, brown; legs and feet, flesh colour.

Field characters.—The tree-pipit can be distinguished from the skylark, which it somewhat resembles, by its more slender build and sprightly movements. It frequents wooded districts or orchards with tall trees around, and sloping banks covered with scrub. Song distinct and described in chapter.

THE MEADOW - PIPIT.

Description.—Length, 5·5 inches. Upper parts, dark brown, with an olive tinge; tail, dark brown; under parts, dull white, with dark brown spots on the throat and breast; bill, dark brown; eyes, dark brown; legs and feet, light brown.

THE ROCK-PIPIT.

Description.—Length, 6·5 inches. Upper parts, olive brown, with darker streaks on back feathers; wings, dark brown; tail, dark brown, with grey margin on outer tail feathers; under parts, buff-yellow, with dark brown streaks on the throat and breast; bill, brown; eyes, brown; legs and feet, brown.

Field characters.—The field characters of the meadow-pipit and rock-pipit are similar. The meadow-pipit has pure white outer tail feathers, while in rock-pipit these are grey, and this is a distinguishing mark in flight. The rock-pipit is also larger. Songs of both birds are similar.

In my chapter on the willow - warbler I mentioned that the meadow-pipit competes with it as being the commonest bird in the country during the summer months. We find the rock-pipit spread under the toe of my shoe; I had stepped on the tail and the bird had flown away without it! In about half an hour's time the pipit was back upon her eggs and, I hope, succeeded in hatching them without further mishaps.

INDEX

Index

Index

Index

Owl, brown, 116

Partridge, 157
Periscope in hide, 34, 35
Philomela, 13
PIPITS—
  Description, 197
  distribution, 197–198
  eggs—
    meadow-, rock-, tree-, 199
  Field Characters, 197
  meadow-, 75, 81, 83
  migration, arrival, tree-, 198
  nest—
    meadow-, rock-, tree-, 199
  song—
    meadow-, tree-, 198–199
  territory, 198

Raven, 147
Redwing, 124
Reed-warbler, 87, 90, 92

ROBIN, 25
  alarm note, 159
  courtship, 157–159
  Description, 155
  distribution, 155
  eggs, 156
  feeding young, 159
  Field Characters, 155
  fighting, 157–159, 161
  incubation, 159
  nest, 156
  own weight of food, 104
  resemblance to nightingale, 160
  song, 160
  territory, 155

SEDGE - WARBLER, 15, 26, 41, 81

SEDGE-WARBLER (*cont.*):
  Description, 87
  eggs, 89
  feeding young, 91
  Field Characters, 87
  incubation, 90
  migration, arrival, 87
  nest, 89
    dummy, 92
  song, 90
    distinction from nightingale's, 91
  territory, 87–89
Singing with food in beak, 33
SKYLARK and WOODLARK—
  courtship, 172
  Description, 169
  eggs, 173
  enemies, 174
  Field Characters, 169
  migration, arrival, 175
  nest, 173
  song—
    sky-, 169, 172
    wood-, 171
  territory, 172
SONG - THRUSH, 26, 34, 41, 81, 132
  bravery, 106
  cockroach, incident with, 105
  Description, 95
  distribution, 96, 97
  eggs, 102
  Field Characters, 95
  fisherman's song, 96
  in Hebrides, 97
  nest, 101
  song—
    distinction from blackbird, 97
    distinction from nightingale, 99
    variation in, 107
  territory, 99
  young, 102, 103
    learning to catch worms, 103

206

Index

Index